SAPPHO:]FRAGMENTS

Before you start to read this book, take this moment to think about making a donation to punctum books, an independent non-profit press,

@ https://punctumbooks.com/support/

If you're reading the e-book, you can click on the image below to go directly to our donations site. Any amount, no matter the size, is appreciated and will help us to keep our ship of fools afloat. Contributions from dedicated readers will also help us to keep our commons open and to cultivate new work that can't find a welcoming port elsewhere. Our adventure is not possible without your support.
Vive la open-access.

Fig. 1. Hieronymus Bosch, Ship of Fools (1490–1500)

HIC SVNT MONSTRA

Sappho

]fragments

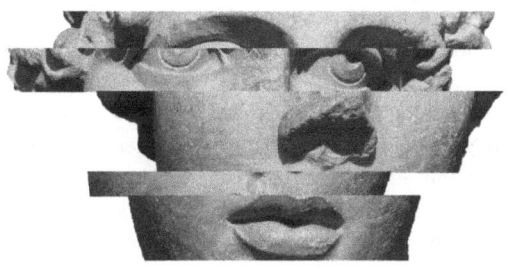

JONATHAN GOLDBERG

with an afterword by
L.O. Aranye Fradenburg Joy

SAPPHO:]FRAGMENTS. Copyright © 2018 Jonathan Goldberg. This work carries a Creative Commons BY-NC-SA 4.0 International license, which means that you are free to copy and redistribute the material in any medium or format, and you may also remix, transform, and build upon the material, as long as you clearly attribute the work to the authors and editors (but not in a way that suggests the authors or punctum books endorses you and your work), you do not use this work for commercial gain in any form whatsoever, and that for any remixing and transformation, you distribute your rebuild under the same license. http://creativecommons.org/licenses/by-nc-sa/4.0/

First published in 2018 by dead letter office, BABEL Working Group, an imprint of punctum books, Earth, Milky Way.
www.punctumbooks.com

The BABEL Working Group is a collective and desiring-assemblage of scholar–gypsies with no leaders or followers, no top and no bottom, and only a middle. BABEL roams and stalks the ruins of the post-historical university as a multiplicity, a pack, looking for other roaming packs with which to cohabit and build temporary shelters for intellectual vagabonds. We also take in strays.

ISBN-13: 978-1-947447-97-4 (print)
ISBN-13: 978-1-947447-98-1 (ePDF)

LCCN: 2018967623
Library of Congress Cataloging Data is available from the Library of Congress

Book design: Kristen McCants
Cover design: Vincent W.J. van Gerven Oei
Cover image: "Portrait of the Poetess Sappho," Roman bust, Archaeological Museum of Istanbul. Photograph by Eric Gaba (2013).

Fragments

1. Sappho — 15
2. γλυκύπικρον — 21
3. Love Revealed — 27
4. *Living as a Lesbian* — 35
5. *Histoire de Sapho* — 43
6. Chance Meetings — 49
7. "*Sapho* to *Philaenis*" — 59
8. *The Country of the Pointed Firs* — 67
9. *Carol* — 75
10. "To begin with Sappho" — 89
11. The Bechdel Test — 107
12. "The Wise Sappho" — 115
13. Sister Outsider — 125
Afterword: After-Party: Sappho Meets Freud — 133
    by L.O. Aranye Fradenburg Joy
Bibliography — 149

Acknowledgments

Eileen Joy invited me to write a book for her punctum books Dead Letter Office series; indeed, it was she who suggested its title would be *Sappho*. I thank her for the provocation and the pleasure I took in fulfilling this assignment. At punctum I am grateful also to Vincent W.J. van Gerven Oei for the cover design and for so expeditiously answering queries and launching the book. Kristen McCants did exemplary copyediting, unobtrusive and always attentive.

I thank Tesla Cariani for some preliminary research on an image that proved unattainable. Dagmawi Woubshet and I exchanged a useful email on *Zami*. I am grateful for advice from Adam Haslett and Daniel Thomas Davis, from Bonnie Honig, Kevin Pask and Marcie Frank. Friends upon whose work I depended kindly endorsed the uses to which I put it: Karen Newman, Robert Reid-Pharr, Laurie Shannon. Lynne Huffer and Sharon Cameron each read a section of this book and responded in gratifying ways. Michael Moon read it all over and again at every stage. To him, as ever, my debts and love only increase. Eve Kosofsky Sedgwick comes first and last in this book, and rightly so; her thinking encompasses mine. I only wish she were still alive to share this one, or that I might once again have been in touch with Michelle Cliff about the ways her work has inspired mine.

Without mostly believing or declaring themselves to be women, they are precocious in seeking out and meditating over transsexual stories, as if sure that those carry some personal message if only it can be divined.... They are often gerontophilic: sharing a grandmother's bedroom, hanging out...with the nuns. What is certain is that they find ways of spending time with women, whether their contemporaries or older, including their mothers and aunts.... Their interest is increasingly in the women themselves, especially lesbians and proto-lesbians, an interest in resources that women and girls can confer — while the boys' sexual attraction may indeed prove to be toward other men.... Maybe not surprisingly, redefining identities and fooling with gender categories provide lifelong, tonic, and challenging nurturance....

    Eve Kosofsky Sedgwick, "Anality: *News from the Front*"

1

Sappho

To begin to suggest what this book will do, it might be best to compare it with another recent book, also titled *Sappho*, that perhaps better fulfills the expectations that title may raise. I have in mind *Sappho*, by Page duBois, Distinguished Professor of Classics and Comparative Literature at the University of California San Diego.[1] DuBois, author of a previous book on Sappho (*Sappho is Burning*—a title, she notes in her acknowledgments, she owes to Judith/Jack Halberstam[2]) and the collaborator with John Daley on an edition of translations of the fragments, is an obvious choice to write a book in the "Understanding Classics" series to which it belongs. Unlike me, she is an expert in the field; her volume seeks to let readers know what can be known through the name "Sappho." To the degree that it is possible, duBois provides information—about the life of Sappho, the corpus of her work, and the transmission of these archaic Greek texts as they were received in antiquity, in

1 All parenthetical citations in this chapter are from Page duBois, *Sappho* (London: I.B. Tauris, 2015). For another queer take on the reception history of Sappho, see Terry Castle, "Always the Bridesmaid, Never the Groom," in *Boss Ladies, Watch Out! Essays on Women, Sex, and Writing*, 167–79 (New York: Routledge, 2002), inspired by Yopie Prins, *Victorian Sappho* (Princeton, NJ: Princeton University Press, 1999). For an early tally of twentieth-century women writers engaged with Sappho, see Susan Gubar, "Sapphistries," *Signs: Journal of Women in Culture and Society* 10, no. 1 (Autumn 1984): 43–62, https://doi.org/10.1086/494113.
2 Page duBois, *Sappho is Burning* (Chicago: University of Chicago Press, 1995), xi.

the classical era, and in more modern times. Her final chapter, "Queer Sappho," is where her project meets mine. Indeed, in seeking to give her readers information, duBois heads in this direction; she offers anything but the concrete knowledge that her topics might lead a reader to expect. The only biography we have of Sappho was written sixteen hundred years after her lifetime. No exact dates for her seventh century BC corpus can be provided, nor is "corpus" really the right word to describe the fragments that we have. Only two or three poems are complete enough to be treated as texts; newly discovered papyri in the last couple of decades have substantiated some biographical information (found in Herodotus) about Sappho and her brothers and filled in the glimpses of herself in old age found in some fragments. They hold out the possibility of more discoveries in years to come. The two texts of Sappho most frequently discussed are Fragment 31, almost all of which is cited as exemplary in Longinus, and the initial poem to Aphrodite that was not printed until the sixteenth century.

How Sappho was known in antiquity (Plato, for instance, alludes to her in the *Phaedrus* and named her as the tenth Muse) stands at some distance from the figure conveyed in the classical era (Ovid, in the *Amores,* penned an anguished letter from Sappho to her male lover Phaon; Catullus translated Fragment 31, substituting himself for Sappho as the presumed speaker in that poem), as well as from being the figure of all sorts of erotic distress she bears in modernity. Compiling the various accounts of Sappho that survive from antiquity, duBois concludes about them that "we will never know" how true any of them might be (80). "What do we make of the appearance of Sappho in [classical] comedy," where she is the object of ridicule for unbridled heterosexual love, duBois asks, and answers, "Difficult to know" (93). "There is no stable 'Sappho,' no fixed person, no knowable biography, no final set of 'collected works'" (153), she concludes, before turning to "Queer Sappho" for the possibilities that lie beyond the supposed certainties of the stable, the fixed, the known. That is where my *Sappho* is situated.

It also is where duBois situates hers. Her opening sentences pronounce Sappho a "figure," "no longer a person" ("a person perhaps," she puts it a bit later [5]), "not yet an author," "a somewhat enigmatic name," "a nexus" of "knowledge, attachment and projection." "Who or what is Sappho" (33), duBois asks, and seeks to give as full an answer as possible to the unanswerable question. In subtitling my book "Fragments," I demure from pursuit of the goal of some kind of complete or absolute knowledge, and do not do what duBois attempts in her chapter 4, "Trying to Translate Sappho," to list everyone from John Donne to Ezra Pound who attempted translations (among them, Katherine Philips, Aphra Behn, Michael Field, H.D., Monique Wittig, and Judy Grahn, to sample the list of female sapphists mentioned). The aim of duBois' book is to tell her readers everything that can be known or has been said in the name of Sappho without the definitive delivery that such an exhaustive empirical gathering might aim to provide. My book does not pretend to that kind of knowledge. I hope that by surveying examples that answer in one way or another to the "figure" of Sappho to further the project of what can be said when the hope of empirical knowledge as truth is abandoned. As duBois shows, for example, it is not even the case that we know what Sappho's words mean; in some cases, we cannot know what words are to be read in texts that don't separate one word from another. In the first fragment, as duBois demonstrates in a close reading, we cannot tell when another voice — presumably that of the Aphrodite being addressed — enters the text; it enters in an indeterminate relationship of identity and difference to the speaking voice who either is addressed as "Sappho" or addresses herself in that name (8). DuBois provides a literal translation of the final line of the penultimate stanza of the poem, "And if he/she/it will love, even not willing" (28). "He/she/it" is as definitive as the poem gets at this moment when the desired object spoken of throughout the poem is about to acquire the female gender that finally is offered through a verbal ending that matches the alpha-privative that earlier proclaimed Aphrodite's deathlessness in a privative form that nonetheless includes the death it denies her (10, 28). Until its final lines, the poem fails to specify the eros it speaks (to he/she/it) even as it appears that a woman named Sappho is addressing a goddess named Aphrodite about a woman she desires. As duBois says, the subject of the poem (and of all the fragments?) is "desire embodied in female form" (12).

This "embodiment" remains at once figurative and figured. It takes place in language, as is intimated in a comedy by Antiphanes, when the Sappho in that text sets a riddle about a woman whose voiceless progeny is nonetheless capable of being heard everywhere. The answer to the riddle about what this progeny might be is that "the feminine being is a written message,...the offspring are the letters..." (92–93). The riddle — the enigma — that "Sappho" poses appears, for example, when, in "Sapho to Philaenis," "Donne restores to Sappho the eros of lesbianism" (117) denied her by Ovid or Catullus, or by classical playwrights, not to mention the numerous writers of modernity who associate the name "Sappho" with a tragic heterosexuality: "Donne, taking on the voice of Sappho as Catullus once did, engages in a transvestism, a transgendering, as he imagines himself not to be Catullus replacing Sappho's speaker, but rather as the woman herself, imagining love-making with another woman" (118). Is Donne thereby "like" Catullus or unlike the Roman poet when he made Sappho's voice his voice and made her desire for a woman his? Is the desire Donne voices in "Sapho to Philaenis" lesbian desire? Is Donne "a 'male lesbian'" (126), a phrase duBois uses not about him but in reference to Swinburne's "Anactoria" and "Sapphics"? If Catullus and Donne each perform acts of "poetic transvestism" (105), what did Sappho do when, in the matrix of Homeric figuration, she turned his tropes of war into hers of love? DuBois cautions that the fragment to Aphrodite does not end by giving "Sappho" her beloved, but by forcing into submission the "he/she/it" who becomes a "she." No feminine–feminine equivalence is on offer in this poem, no mutuality or mirroring identification is being held out in this hostage situation, except perhaps a shared suffering, inflicted. But was the Homeric matrix in which Sappho made her intervention only one of male domination?[3] Is that the

---

3 For a stunning essay that works from that supposition to possibilities of female–female erotic expression within the Homeric matrix, see Jack Winkler, "Gardens of Nymphs: Public and Private in Sappho's Lyrics," in *Reflections of Women in Antiquity*, edited by Helene

relation of Achilleus and Patrokles in *The Iliad*? DuBois seems to caution against a sappy sapphism that would turn Sappho into a version of the lesbian writer that she likens to "Lesbian lesbians" exemplified by H.D. and Bryher (128).

Instead, duBois reads Sappho along with her fellow "Lesbian, Alkaios" (2, 33; "Lesbian Alkaios" 43), Lesbians both, but not the same, as can be seen in the ways they depict the figure of Homer's Helen; she is rehabilitated by Sappho in an effort duBois compares to Plato's attempt to redefine the good (45), although duBois also wants Sapphic embodiment to be differentiated from platonic philosophical idealism while at the same time seeing how close the account of eros in the *Phaedrus* is to Fragment 31's depiction of desire (95–96). Are lesbians Lesbians? Only for Monique Wittig, duBois avers (157). Yet it was also Wittig who insisted that lesbians aren't women, since "woman" is a concept whose meaning is derivative of and dependent on the male / female gender system. Wittig and Sande Zeig's page on Sappho in their dictionary of *Lesbian People* is a blank, not only because the question of who or what Sappho is cannot be answered by the facts that are missing and the texts we don't have, but because Sappho baffles the categorical when it comes to sex and gender and sexuality.[4] DuBois is impatient with a certain elegiac strain in queer theory that can read backwards only in pain and anguish and under the sign of loss. For her, the past — as in the figure of Sappho — is a site of possibility: "one might reconsider the possibilities inherent in looking backwards differently. That is, looking backward not just to the suffering and depression of gay and lesbian and queer persecution, but also to the model of an ancient world in which the structures of heterosexual norms, punishment, confession and secrecy had not yet been instituted in the name of the one god" (170). Those sentences inspire the ones that follow.

P. Foley, 63–90 (New York: Gordon and Breach Science Publishers, 1981).

4   Monique Wittig and Sande Zeig, *Lesbian People: Material for a Dictionary* (London: Virago, 1980).

2

γλυκύπικρον

I read Anne Carson's acclaimed 1986 book *Eros the Bittersweet* for the first time only when I began working on this book.[1] I have come to see it as invaluable, although I was initially disappointed. With the exception of a single quotation from Jacques Lacan, Carson's book does not register overtly the kinds of theoretical thinking that was certainly ready-to-hand in the 1980s for literary critics and writers with a philosophical bent of mind like hers. This absence worried me, since connections between eros and writing are central to Carson; such connections, worked through especially in texts by Derrida, seem quite germane to Carson's project, yet she ignores his critique of phonocentrism. Arguing that a recognizable western version of desire only began when the Greeks started writing, Carson attaches this discovery to dualistic pairings—oral/written, immediate/distant—that seem ripe for deconstruction. However, by reading the book through that lens, the absence of a theoretical vocabulary seemed ultimately not to matter. Carson's focus on the coincidence of eros and writing is amenable to a recognition that there is no *hors-texte*.

The other issue that first perturbed me seemed less easily surmounted, the sidestepping of any discussion of gender and sexuality; *à la greque*, Carson supposes heterosexuality and pederasty are the two forms that desire takes, and not just for the Greeks: among the modern texts glanced at to universalize the Greek discovery of eros, Carson cites Virginia Woolf's

1 All parenthetical citations are from Anne Carson, *Eros the Bittersweet* (London: Dalkey Archive Press, 1998).

The Waves for a moment of male–male love in it. Lesbian desire seems not to exist.

Nonetheless, crucially, Carson is arguing from a word — γλυκύπικρον, *glukupikron*, "sweet bitter" — that is apparently an invention of Sappho's; the fact of its invention opens Carson's book, and it appears in Fragment 130, Sappho's decisive initiation of the western discourse of desire as bittersweet, desire as a divided, doubled, self-contradictory state. Fragment 130 in Carson's translation reads: "Eros once again limb-loosener whirls me / sweetbitter, impossible to fight off, creature stealing up" (3).[2] Carson's book about eros is a book about Sappho, about the language for eros she created. The pairing of love and writing — the writing of love that is eros — is, in other words, sapphic. What appears to be universalized and generalized in the book is nonetheless sapphic love, love as sapphic.[3]

Discussion of Fragment 31, one of the two Sappho poems that seem almost complete, recurs throughout *Eros the Bittersweet*. To summarize this well-known verse: a man is seen sitting and listening to a woman who is speaking and laughing: "he seems to me equal to gods," the poem opens (12). He is unlike the poet who, recording this scene, describes poetic debility — inability

---

2 I cite here the translations that appear in *Eros the Bittersweet*. Elsewhere I cite Sappho as translated by Carson in *If Not, Winter: Fragments of Sappho* (New York: Vintage Books, 2003), checking her poetic renderings against the standard Loeb Classical Library prose translations found in *Greek Lyric I: Sappho and Alcaeus*, translated by David A. Campbell (Cambridge, MA: Harvard University Press, 1982).

3 Lisa L. Moore comes to something like the same premise in "A Lesbian History of the Sonnet," *Critical Inquiry* 43, no. 4 (Summer 2017): 813–38, https://doi.org/10.1086/692380, a point vitiated by elementary formal and historical confusions: the volta of the Petrarchan sonnet is not identical to the paradoxes Sappho entertains in her sapphics; nor are Petrarch's *rime sparse* "sonnet sequences to unattainable Beatrice" (818); nor did Milton write "a handful of sonnets, some in Latin" (826). These confusions are related to the gender confusion (transgendering) that Moore reads as male encroachments upon lesbian desire as the secret history of the sonnet.

γλυκύπικρον

to speak, to see, to hear — sweating and shaking: "I am dead — or almost / I seem to me" (13). A poem whose opening suggests it will be about a man and a woman, in which he is capable of some godlike imperturbability before the entrancing woman, turns into a poem about the relation of the figure that Carson first calls "the poet" (13), as I have been, following her to this scene, to this woman speaking and laughing. What matters for Carson here and throughout the discussion that follows is the triangulation of the scenario. She treats this distantiation as akin to the effect of writing, but also as a way of describing the act of thinking: the epigraph to the section of the book in which Fragment 31 is first discussed is from the inscription over the door of Plato's Academy: "Let no one enter here who is ignorant of geometry" (12). The abstracting and generalizing that *Eros the Bittersweet* reads from this scene of poetic triangulation would seem to be in the service of an idealizing that moots any gendered or erotic specificity to sapphic desire.

This turns out not to be the case, however, the next time Carson turns to Fragment 31; just like the poet in Fragment 130 who again and again encounters love as sweetbitter, Carson returns to the scene of writing eros to plumb its unfathomable recursive depths. "If we look carefully at a lover in the midst of desire, for example Sappho in her Fragment 31, we see how severe an experience for her is confrontation with the beloved even at a distance. Union would be annihilating" (62). The addition of a gendered adjective, the identification of "the poet" as Sappho, begins to suggest that these specifications are not merely incidental to this poem, that Carson's "for example" is exemplary, not a casual, chance instance. Carson's first, generalized discussion of the poem, and her second closer look, in which gendered identity is acknowledged, spaces the contradiction at the heart of her analysis. Love is bittersweet — bitter and sweet; what is desired, and in order for it to remain as desired, must never be had. Having would annihilate eros. When the generic poet becomes the gendered Sappho, when the desire in question is sapphic, eros becomes, by definition, and not just by chance, rooted in female same-sex desire. The stunning claim is that wherever and however eros originates, this is its point of origin for anyone.

Following Lacan, but also Plato, the desire that Carson traces from the exemplary Fragment 31 — the desire of the poet / woman — is the realization of a lack impossible to fulfill (a lack one does not desire to fill). It is the beginning of something structured never to end. It takes one out of oneself to places one has never gone before, precisely through the loss of self awakened by desire. This loss is a matter of gain since it entails the realization of something outside oneself that is constituted in the shattering of the self. The realization ignited by the lover (Sappho is burning) is not only about her, but about something that exceeds the very connection that is made by desire.

"Remember the structure of Sappho's Fragment 31," Carson insists as she pulls the threads of her argument together, again by way of the same poem. "Eros is always a story in which lover, beloved and the difference between them interact. The interaction is a fiction arranged by the mind of the lover. It carries an emotional charge both hateful and delicious and emits a light like knowledge. No one took a more clear-eyed view of this matter than Sappho" (169). Carson compares this "matter" to a "charge" that she describes as electric, some elemental energy. By the end of her book this Sapphic knowledge is equivalent to Socratic love (philosophy is the love of wisdom rooted in its profound lack). "A power to see the difference between what is known and what is unknown constitutes Sokrates' wisdom and motivated his searching life" (172). The godlike man in Fragment 31 may be godlike because he can be in this place of betweenness, of a knowing not knowing, a having not having, or because he has attained the impossible. What would that be? On the one hand, it is something beyond the doublebind of the bittersweet that nonetheless remains bittersweet. It is the fulfillment of the "action of reaching out toward a meaning not yet known...a reach that never quite arrives, bittersweet" (166): so Carson defines the projects of both Sappho and of Sokrates. It may be akin to (identical to) the Lacanian enigma that Carson first cites: "Desire...evokes lack of being under the three figures of the nothing that constitutes the basis of the demand for love, of the hate that even denies the other's being, and of the unspeakable element in that which is ignored in its request" (11). This Lacanian dictum, this enigma, is echoed in

γλυκύπικρον

the quotation Carson provides from Shakespeare's *The Winter's Tale* 1.2.137ff. that serves as the epigraph for the final chapter in *Eros the Bittersweet*. "Affection," it begins, "With what's unreal thou coactive art, / And fellow'st nothing."

"Fellow'st" could mean "creates" (in a biological sense, makes something that is nothing), but it could just as easily mean that affect creates a fellow coactively, creating a phantasmatic other; this simulacrum in the mind, made in adversive desiring, can be imagined as another body that might yet be thought to be an image of one's own; it is the image of what one lacks to be. This nothing that is — that is the poem — also is an image of an impossibility-to-be that is the difference between Being and beings (to phrase triangulated eros now in Heideggerian terms). The female–female desire that goes unnamed in Carson's *Eros the Bittersweet* has a name that is not one: Sappho, sapphism. It exceeds the usual binarism of gender since this female–female eros is not a matter of the same.

3

Love Revealed

The first room in the Tate Britain show *Queer British Art 1861–1967* (April 5–October 1, 2017) was labeled "Coded Desires." That rubric, in fact, pretty much summarized the curatorial guidance throughout the exhibit. The placard accompanying Simeon Solomon's 1864 watercolor *Sappho and Erinna in a Garden at Mytilene* (Fig. 1) informed viewers that "Sappho is associated with the island of Lesbos and her story gives us the word 'lesbian.'" (True enough, Sappho did come from Lesbos, but anyone who comes from Lesbos is a Lesbian, not necessarily a lesbian; even Sappho — her story — has not been thought to have been one for much of her history.) We are told next that Swinburne may have influenced Solomon's choice of subject matter. How does that follow? Was Swinburne's sapphism the same as hers? As Solomon's? Does male art constitute sapphism? It could seem so, but the text continues in a different (opposite?) direction: "While female same-sex desire was considered more acceptable than its male equivalent, Solomon's depiction of Sappho's fervent kiss and Erinna's swooning response is unusually explicit and the image was not publically exhibited." So, has Solomon punctured acceptability by showing a coded non-sapphic, that is, male–male desire? Is the fervency of his desire for men coded as unacceptable female–female desire? Does "female same-sex desire" stand in a relation of equivalence to male–male desire, which thus enables this coding, or is the opposite the case, as the label first posited? We read on to the next contradictory sentence: "Yet for most people, there seems to have been little sense that certain sexual practices or forms of gender expression reflected a core aspect of the self. Instead,

Figure 1. Simeon Solomon, *Sappho and Erinna in a Garden at Mytilene* (1864)

this was a world of fluid possibilities." If so, why did such fluidity come to a halt, what boundary did Solomon violate that kept this artwork from public display? He "attracted sustained criticism of 'unwholesomeness' or 'effeminacy,'" we are finally told. For what? This image?

Was Solomon drawn to lesbian representation as a coded expression of a male–male equivalent that also would have overturned gendered distinctions? What made this image intolerable, incapable of public display? Is it really as "frank" as all that? The passionate kiss seems to be delivered into the air; lips do not meet lips. Possibly Erinna is restraining Sappho, not swooning. Such an image would still be sapphic, indeed, bittersweet, but not in being fervent and graphic, rather, in its non-consummation.

Is it a fact that the image was not displayed? According to the catalogue Colin Cruise edited for the Birmingham Museum and Art Gallery show, "Love Revealed: Simeon Solomon and the Pre-Raphaelites" (October 1, 2005–January 15, 2006), Solomon's image was displayed in the Goupil Gallery in 1896, a number of years after it was painted, but still in Solomon's lifetime.[1]

Solomon depicted Sappho a number of times. The Birmingham catalogue includes a drawing of her face identical to her face in the watercolor; she is represented alone. That may account for the possibility that in the watercolor, too, the two women are not in a fervid relationship. Another image by Solomon of Sappho and Erinna in the Birmingham show depicts Erinna with a man, Sappho apparently being rejected, an image that might have been inspired by Fragment 31. Rejection is part of the experience of sapphic love, indeed, constitutive of it. Of these images of Sappho, Cruise avers, "She appears to represent all same-sex desire and Solomon's own sexual feelings" (112). What is "and" doing in this sentence—affirming Solomon's desire as a kind of same-sex desire or differentiating it? The possibility that Solomon wants to represent all desire as sapphic in his watercolor may be suggested by the diminutive statue of Aphrodite on the right side of the image; the figure seems to be countenancing the relation between Sappho and Erinna. This statue may be inspired by the first fragment, addressed to Aphrodite. In it the voice of the goddess of love—any love—becomes indistinguishable from the voice invoking her and making known a desire that has, finally, a woman as its object, something not clear until almost the end of the poem (the boundary between voices remains indeterminate).

Solomon was sometimes lambasted by art critics for unmanliness; he was also highly praised. Walter Pater, for example, in an essay on Dionysius, seeking to complicate the notion that the god simply stands for inebriate excess, singles out an image of Bacchus by Solomon to advance his argument: "[I]n a *Bacchus* by a young Hebrew painter, in the exhibition of the Royal Academy of 1868, there was a complete and very fascinating

1 The catalogue is included in Colin Cruise, *Love Revealed: Simeon Solomon and the Pre-Raphaelites* (London: Merrell, 2005). See 134 for information on the commission and the history of the exhibition of the image. However, in an essay in that volume, Elizabeth Prettejohn, "Solomon's Classicism," 39–45, claims that the image was not displayed (43).

realisation of such a motive; the god of the bitterness of wine, 'of things too sweet'; the sea-water of the Lesbian grape become somewhat brackish in the cup."[2] Dionysius is a "dual god" for Pater, "almost identical with Demeter." Rather than decoding one figure as another, Pater insists on the paradox of sapphic bittersweet erotics, self-shattering loss coupled with maternal solicitude. He sees this sapphism realized in the figure of Bacchus.

* * *

Among our contemporaries, no one has been more vocal than Neil Bartlett in his appreciation of Simeon Solomon. There are three versions of theatrical pieces entitled *A Vision of Love Revealed in Sleep*—Bartlett takes his title from an 1871 prose poem by Solomon himself. Cruise notes that this poem's sources include the *Song of Songs,* Dante, the *Roman de la Rose,* and the *Hypnerotomachia Poliphili*; if, as he says, "the book is now regarded as an important early defense of male–male desire" (158), it achieves that aim through a literary tradition that doesn't so readily answer to that agenda. (What "codes" what?) The 1987 version of Bartlett's piece appears in *Solo Voices*. Bartlett reprised it for a single performance for the Tate show on 7 July 2017. It was originally performed by Bartlett in the nude, "shaved and powdered—a marble statue, an artist's model, a painting"; his solo voice is embodied but in a form that seems to make it a statue, a work of visual art.[3] In his note accompanying the text, Bartlett describes the piece as employing "various kinds of garrulous, high or low, outraged or outrageous, theatrical effeminacy—both male and female." This first version of the piece expresses, as Bartlett claims, his own homosexuality, but it is not something simply manifest in his naked body (powdered and shaved, it is not simply his body on view). And although it is a solo performance, it was scarcely univocal; as

---

2 Walter Pater, *Greek Studies: A Series of Essays* (London: Macmillan, 1911), 42.
3 Neil Bartlett, *Solo Voices: Monologues 1987–2004* (London: Oberon Books, 2005). I cite from the 2013 unpaginated electronic edition.

he says, the voices we hear are not exactly his own; rather, he is taking "dictation...impelled by the sound of imagined voices." Music accompanies the voice (these voices), Schoenberg and Kate Bush at first, while, towards the close, he describes the monologist (himself?) "morphing into a drunken impersonation of early Tina Turner," before ending with a medley of songs famously sung by the early twentieth-century vaudevillian Marie Lloyd, including among them "The Boy I love is up in the gallery." At the end of this version of the piece (this occurs in the later versions as well), an imagined letter from Simeon Solomon is delivered and read aloud. When it is displayed, it is shown to be a piece of blank paper. The text is not so much a code to be deciphered as it is a void filled with potential.

In the final version of Bartlett's stage piece, first performed in 1989 and revived a year later, the solo performer, called Neil, was joined by Three Queens, originally Bette Bourne, Regina Fong, and Ivan. The original monologue, a solo voice doing voices, was extended to these other voices, not that each of these drag queens spoke in a singular voice, nor is one identical to the other; each has its (his/her) own production style. In the preface to this later version, Bartlett remarks that "it is always better to tell your own story by telling someone else's."[4] Solomon provides text and subject for the actors and the author (whatever that category means in these circumstances); they are all themselves always in character (whatever that means). Indeed, the text inspiring these texts — Simeon Solomon's *A Vision of Love Revealed in Sleep* — is haunted, and not only by its precursor texts. It involves an I's encounter with another who is his Soul, and who serves as his guide in a search that ends in an annihilating union: "made one with the Heart of Love, its inmost, secret flame: my spirit was wholly swallowed up, and I knew no more."[5] Once again, Sappho is burning. Solomon

---

4 Neil Bartlett, *A Vision of Love Revealed in Sleep (Part Three)*, is included in *Gay Plays*, edited by Michael Wilcox, Volume 4, 87–112 (London: Methuen Drama, 1990). I cite from Bartlett's preface, 84. Bartlett fulfills that dictum too in *Who Was That Man? A Present for Mr Oscar Wilde* (London: Serpent's Tale, 1988).

5 I cite Solomon's text from Simon Reynolds, *The Vision of Simeon*

represents this as the union of Bride and Bridegroom, turning the trope of the *Song of Solomon* in an allegorical direction not quite congruent with how the Church handled that text to make its sexuality acceptable, but not entirely dissimilar either.

In a review of the 2005–2006 Birmingham show that he wrote for *The Guardian*[6] — his most recent response to Simeon Solomon — Bartlett pauses over two images. "Love in Autumn" conjures the vision Solomon wrote; Bartlett sees it as the visual equivalent to Lord Alfred Douglas's dream vision that concludes "I am the love that dare not speak its name."[7] The figure of Love in Solomon's image is a pink-winged nude whose genitals are covered by the windswept drapery of a Botticelli nymph. The face and figure resembles that of Eric, Count Stenbock, as Solomon described him: "[H]is appearance was that of a tall, graceful intellectual looking girl and although not exactly good-looking, his eye and expression are very beautiful." Another early image that fascinates Bartlett shows a Jewish wedding ceremony: bride and groom are framed by two male figures, a "pouting" boy regarded with "tender seriousness" by a would-be suitor. This juxtaposition of joined and separated, cross-gender and same-gender couples anticipates the end of Solomon's prose poem whose bridal figuration combines what this wedding image separates and juxtaposes. The effect is something that John Addington Symonds noted of Solomon's painted figures more generally: "[T]hey have the sorrow of those who have no cause for sorrow except that they are as they are in a world not made after their pattern…These faces are without sex…" (quoted in Reynolds, 25). Symonds might have come to the same conclusion from Solomon's prose poem; its vision of

---

Solomon (Stroud: Catalpa Press, 1984), 79.
6 "Fallen Angel," *The Guardian*, October 7, 2005, https://www.theguardian.com/artanddesign/2005/oct/08/art.
7 For the text of "Two Loves," I quote from Brian Reade's anthology *Sexual Heretics: Male Homosexuality in English Literature from 1850 to 1900* (London: Routledge and Kegan Paul, 1970), 362; this is also the source for my quotations of Solomon's 1886 letter describing Eric, Count Stenbock, 37.

"Love imprisoned in an alien land of oblivion" (66) is akin to "a world not made after their pattern" he invokes.

Bartlett ends his *Guardian* piece with the images Solomon made at the end of his life. This also is the trajectory followed in his theatrical work. Solomon's ruin as an artist followed his arrest — he was caught having sex in a public lavatory. His supporters (Swinburne, Burne-Jones) fled; he was alienated from his family. He wound up living in the poorhouse, drawing in chalk on sidewalks. In "Fallen Angel," Bartlett asks: "[W]as the arrest in fact Solomon's making rather than his undoing?" He answers that question in the final version of his theatrical spectacle when he insists "And he never never never never apologized for what he had done." Stripped of all social support (such as it had been), his last works abandon the extravagance of his earlier art: "All that is left of his earlier repertoire of androgynous posturing is a handful of simple dream-like images," often of "pairs of faces" side by side, or of a single face drawn to itself. Solomon "found his true subject — the introspective mind," Bartlett avers. This is the place that leads to thinking otherwise. "By the end, the faces are not just androgynous, they are sexless, impersonal, living in a lonely realm of shame and hunger, of desire and dreams." Pater had commended the melancholy of Bacchus because Solomon's figure incorporated a bitter sweetness whose impersonality had everything to do with the occupation of an extra-personal identity. That is why in *A Vision of Love Revealed in Sleep* the Soul is outside the Self, its other, its image, its companion. That is why, too, this division of the Same refuses the category of gender.

In Bartlett's original theater piece, androgyny is homosexuality. In the final version, this is enacted, embodied by the Queens who join Neil to voice Solomon's vision. That play in fact begins by insisting that a vision is precisely what is not seen (that's what makes it a vision). "Vision: Something which is apparently seen otherwise than by ordinary sight" — as in a dream. Indeed, we say of someone dreamy, it's a vision (*Gay Plays* 87). Solomon's final drawings, Bartlett avers, are "perhaps the most truly beautiful work of his strange and troubled life. Looking at these obsessively imagined faces 100 years later, it is hard not to think that their hungers remain unappeased, their dreams still unrealised." Sapphic trajectories. "I felt just like one who sets out on a journey but who doesn't know where the journey is supposed to end," Solomon's dreamer avers in Bartlett's first version of *Love Revealed*. If these texts and images are written in a code, it cannot yet be translated.

4

Living as a Lesbian

My heading titles a 1986 volume of Cheryl Clarke's poems, republished in 2014 in the "sapphic classics" series of Sinister Wisdom and A Midsummer Night's Press.[1] "Living as a Lesbian" also is the title of an essay in Robert Reid-Pharr's 2001 *Black Gay Man*.[2] The echo is intended: Reid-Pharr names Clarke on the opening page of his essay (153); he quotes lines from *Living as a Lesbian* several times (on 155, 157, 158, 160, and 161). A mention of "Cheryl" in the context of "dyke parties in Brooklyn" that he attends (157) seems likely to refer to her.[3] "Cheryl phones" (160), looking to borrow money, echoing a situation in "no more encomiums," the poem from *Living as a Lesbian* cited most frequently in Reid-Pharr's essay (the poem recalls an argument with a former lover "over some money I owed her" [54]). "We are a couple," Reid-Pharr writes of himself and Cheryl; they are coupled as well in sharing the phrase "living as a lesbian." "We are a couple, mentioned in one breath as dinner parties are planned, given to public quarrels over the minutiae of everyday

1 All parenthetical citations are from Cheryl Clark, *Living as a Lesbian* (New York: A Midsummer Night's Press; Berkeley, CA: Sinister Wisdom, 2014).
2 All parenthetical citations are from Robert Reid-Pharr, *Black Gay Man: Essays* (New York: New York University Press, 2001).
3 It does not, as Robert Reid-Pharr informed me in an email on May 3, 2018: "One small matter that I think you might want to just ignore. The Cheryl referenced in my piece is, in fact, Cheryl Dunye[,] not Cheryl Clarke herself, but I always liked and provoked the confusion." I am taking Robert's advice, and leaving my significantly erroneous supposition in the text.

life, constantly aware of each other's steps and jealous of the intrusion of outsiders" (160–1). This sounds like the usual use of "couple," and yet: Reid-Pharr refers to their coupling as "our lesbianism" (161). What could that mean as a description of a black gay man and a woman who has identified as a black lesbian since she came out in 1979, and continues to do so, as she affirms in "Lesbianism, 2000"?[4] However, Clarke insists there that "lesbianism has emerged at this time in my life as more of a strategy and less of a hard-and-fixed-identity-politics-that-I-am-going-to-be-no-matter-how-it-gets-deconstructed. One never knows how one may have to 'live as a lesbian'" (383). That statement is, in fact, consistent with what Clarke affirmed in her much-cited 1981 essay "Lesbianism: An Act of Resistance," often taken as an example of fixed identity politics: "There is no one kind of lesbian, no one kind of lesbian behavior, and no one kind of lesbian relationship" (27). Would that affirmation embrace the identification espoused by Reid-Pharr?

A way to approach this question resides, I think, in the "as" of the shared title of Clarke's book of poems and Reid-Pharr's essay. Living as a lesbian is not the same thing as being a lesbian. Clarke's lesbianism seems necessarily attached to her gender if we follow the definition of "lesbian" offered in "Lesbianism: An Act of Resistance": "[A] woman...who says she is" (26). This definition certainly allows great latitude in how one claims "lesbian," but would nonetheless seem to require being a woman as a non-negotiable prerequisite, as much a bottom line as the nominal "man" is in the title of Reid-Pharr's book. Clarke also affirms lesbianism as "an ideological, political, and philosophical means of liberation of all women from heterosexual tyranny" (27). She extends this galvanizing formulation for radical feminism beyond women in her equally much-cited 1983 essay, "The Failure to Transform: Homophobia in the Black Community." There she imagines black gay men and lesbians as threats to and threatened by the heterosexist domination

---

4 All parenthetical citations are from prose and poems not in *Living as a Lesbian* are drawn from Cheryl Clarke, *The Days of Good Looks: The Prose and Poetry of Cheryl Clarke, 1980 to 2005* (New York: Carroll & Graf, 2006).

that characterizes patriarchy in general (and by black men who make such claims in the name of the black community). Clarke reiterates this point in the 2000 essay on lesbianism when she writes that "with the exception of black gay men, black men have not affirmed their solidarity with black women," only to add a caveat, "and even black gay men must continue to check their masculinist tendencies and male privilege" (390). "Feminism still means roughly: the revolution that will liberate all women (and men) from patriarchal oppression" (382).

Reid-Pharr heeds these words as he opens the Coda to his essay:

> *By becoming lesbian I have done nothing more nor less than become myself.*
>
> I had expected to end this piece with these words, forcing all of us, myself included, to reevaluate what it means to be labeled lesbian, gay, straight, bi, transgendered, asexual. And yet this is not enough. For, even as I recognize the difficulty of giving definition and meaning to our various identities, I also realize that as I struggle to lay claim to my lesbianism I am always confronted with the reality of my own masculinity, this strange and complex identity that I continue to have difficulty recognizing as privilege. (162)

This paragraph seems straightforward enough; however, certain echoes in the writing destabilize its crucial terms. How does the "myself" of the italicized sentence relate to the "myself included" of the sentence that follows? The first "myself" is the self one is, or, at least, becomes, while the second "myself" is pluralized, forced, moreover, to confront itself and its presuppositions about itself. This confrontation is staged by the impossibility that a black gay man could become himself as lesbian because of the "reality" of his "own masculinity," yet this "reality" is challenged by the realization that "our various identities" are difficult to define. Is the ability to "recognize" the variousness and variableness of "our...identities" one with the difficulty in "recognizing" masculinity as a privilege when his masculinity also is a strange and complex, non-singular reality? Indeed, who is included in the "our" of "our various identities"? These questions are all about "as," about identifications and the identical when the same word seems to split in two. The resemblance is like that couple constituted by Reid-Pharr's "I" and "Cheryl": "I respect her boyishness as she cherishes my effeminacy. We are a couple" (160) joined through an "as." At least adjectively, they exchange identities that seem substantial, nominative — man / woman — in which gender comes closer to being an "as" than the category at which deconstruction halts.

Reid-Pharr's "Living as a Lesbian" offers an account of how he became a lesbian, though to put it that way errs in suggesting that the essay has a conventional narrative structure. In fact, it loops the way the opening of the Coda does. The initial sentence of the essay, "In 1985 Barbara Smith came like a fresh wind to Chapel Hill" (153), recurs (on 159 and 161) and is the final sentence of the essay. 1985 was, I suppose, the year that 20-year-old Reid-Pharr started college at UNC and heard Smith speak (the "like" that makes the event a simile ushers us into the "as" where the essay exists). She enters the text as text a bit later in the first of several citations of Smith, this one from the Combahee River Collective that Smith had helped found a decade before. (Reid-Pharr cites the manifesto from its printing in *Home Girls: A Black Feminist Anthology,* edited by Smith and published by Kitchen Table Women of Color Press that Smith founded and ran for a number of years; the important anthology *This Bridge Called My Back: Writings of Radical Women of Color* as well as Audre Lorde's *I am Your Sister: Black Women Organizing Across Sexualities* were other crucial Kitchen Table publications.) Reid-Pharr's citation from the Combahee River Collective includes the central goal of the group: "[S]truggling against racial, sexual, heterosexual, and class oppression" (words also cited by Clarke in her essay on lesbianism as resistance [27]); he continues the citation to the end of the sentence, which insists on "the fact that the major systems of oppression are interlocked" (154). "Interlocked," but not identical, joined as with an "as"; so, too, Clarke draws analogies between the oppression of women and class and racial oppression. Because of the interlocking of oppressions, Clarke insists that "all of us have to accept or reject allies on the basis of politics, not on the specious basis of skin color. *Have not black people suffered betrayal from our own people?"* (38).

Reid-Pharr allies his lesbianism with all the women he knows; his litany of names concludes with "Barbara, the mother of us all" (157), a tribute that echoes his mention of Lorde earlier: "Audre Lorde, Audre: Poet, Mother, Sister, Lesbian, Warrior, Cancer Survivor" (155).

The naming of Smith as "mother of us all" (all we home girls) is followed by another citation from her writing. Reid-Pharr alludes to his bookcases and files, filled with *Sinister Wisdom, Black Lesbians* and the like; the gay male writing he owns (most of it porn), he reports, he keeps under his bed. One set of writing is the place to go to think about sexuality, the other is connected to having sex; Reid-Pharr thus ponders whether in the bath house he is "still lesbian": "Is it lesbianism that spills out of the end of my cock as bald-headed men with grizzled beards and homemade tattoos slap my buttocks and laugh triumphantly? Is it lesbianism that allows me to walk these difficult streets alone, afraid only that I will *not* be seen, accosted, 'forced' into sexual adventure?" (162). Perhaps Samuel Delaney's *Motion of Light on Water,* the instigator of Reid-Pharr's first visit to the baths, figures in these questions, along with his wondering whether he is "not lesbian at all, but rather like a drag queen: by day a more or less effeminate, woman-loving gay man, by night a pussy, a buck" (163). "Like" or "as," by day or night, the identities he affirms keep crossing each other.

Reid-Pharr's second citation from Smith alludes to writing by black lesbians who "have found the courage to commit their lives and words to paper" as "miraculous" (157). In the Introduction to the 2014 edition of *Living as a Lesbian,* Alexis Pauline Gumbs writes of a kind of miracle: "even before I read *Living as a Lesbian* I was living inside it" (15). In the afterword to its republication, Clarke comments on the appropriateness of her book becoming a "sapphic classic[]": she had read the classical Sophocles and Euripides early; "Sappho came much, much later, as we contemporary cunnilinguists fashioned our own sapphic verse" (128). Her pun resonates against the citation of the opening stanza from "sexual preference" as it appears in Reid-Pharr's "Living as a Lesbian":

> *I'm a queer lesbian.*
> *Please don't go down on me yet.*
> *I do not prefer cunnilingus.*
> *(There's room for me in the movement.)* (160)

It follows a citation from a poem written by Reid-Pharr; his lover at the time found it objectionable for the line "Like a cat" used to describe a man's sexual position, "Ass lifted toward heaven," but referring as easily grammatically to the I of the poem doing the fucking. "We broke up. I left for the comfort of my girl friends. He started dating women...both...finding our own deepest desires had turned back on themselves" (160). Like. As. Turning back and forward and coinciding.

What does it mean for a gay man to be "living as a lesbian"? For Reid-Pharr it is to be continually in process towards an identity one will never achieve. Clarke points in a similar direction when she uses the phrase "living as a lesbian" over and again to title her poems, recontextualizing the phrase each time (e.g., "living as a lesbian underground: a futuristic fantasy," "living as a lesbian on the make," "living as a lesbian at 35," "living as a lesbian at 45," "living as a lesbian underground fin de siecle"). "Living as a lesbian at 45" recalls "a frequent dream" of sex with a man which lead her to her writing: "and you may have work like poetry/to do like now" (296). This dream corresponds to her life: "In 1973, after four years of reckless heterosexuality, I collided high speed with lesbians and lesbianism" (386). There was a "before I became a lesbian"; in 2000 she is "inclined to embellish this narrative [of before and after] with the fact of my relationship with a jazz-loving, freaky, myopic white boy that helped me cross over the burning sands of group disapproval/dissension" (387). This white boy sounds like one of Reid-Pharr's "favorite sex partners, Rick, an ugly, poor, white trash southerner" (9). "When we are together, we imagine, if only for a moment, a world transformed, a world so incredibly sexy and hot that the stupid, banal, and costly structures of racism, homophobia, poverty, and disease that work to keep us apart become nothing more than dully painful memories from the past" (12).

Living as a lesbian leads Reid-Pharr to the "as" of identifications that create identity that preserve difference at the same time, locations, locutions, in a real that allows for realizations that always put pressure on the real, its categories, its temporality. "What I know for certain is that this self, this lesbian-identified gay man, is in constant flux. I live like a lesbian, *as* a lesbian because I know no better way of life. Still, I live beyond her in a province that continues to be preserved exclusively for men, all the while reaping the many fruits of sexual apartheid" (163). This certainty and this place are rephrased as the essay concludes as "the limitlessness of my boundaries" (163), a paradoxical locution, location ("Mira Loca," 156) that transgresses and affirms the contradiction housed in its key words and encapsulated in an "I" and a "my" that seeks a home, a mother whose breath was "like a fresh wind" or, better, like words on a page.

Cunning linguistics.

"Once *home* was a long way off, a place I had never been to but knew out of my mother's mouth.... There it is said that the desire to lie with other women is a drive from the mother's blood."[5] "In 1985 Barbara Smith came like a fresh wind to Chapel Hill."

---

5 Audre Lorde, *Zami: A New Spelling of My Name* (Freedom, CA: Crossing Press, 1982), 256.

5

Histoire de Sapho

In *Fictions of Sappho, 1546-1937*, Joan DeJean is emphatic about the role that Sappho has played in French literature. 1546 is the date of the first French publication of Sappho's first fragment (in Greek); Louise Labé's 1555 *Oeuvres* — whose initial elegy identifies the author's subject as "l'Amour Lesbienne" — is the initiating text at which DeJean glances to open her history of Sapphic fictions.[1] At the very least, Labé's phrase claims her identity as a poet by way of Sappho's muse. The decisive beginning for DeJean, however, is Madeleine de Scudéry, whose early volume of harangues, *Les Femmes Illustres* (1642), closes with a letter from Sapho to Erinna (Simeon Solomon's watercolor of the two is on the cover of DeJean's book) in which Sapho enjoins Erinna to write. Scudéry's 10-volume romance, *Artamène, ou, Le Grand Cyrus* (1649-53), includes in its final volume the *Histoire de Sapho*. These two texts by Scudéry received their first modern translation into English in Karen Newman's 2003 contribution to the University of Chicago series "The Other Voice in Early Modern Europe."[2] The voice is that of the woman

---

1   See Joan DeJean, *Fictions of Sappho, 1546-1937* (Chicago: University of Chicago Press, 1989), 38-41, for the discussion of Labé. The treatment of Scudéry to which I allude is on 96-110, esp. 104-7. For a text of Labé's first elegy, see her *Complete Prose and Poetry*, edited by Deborah Lesko Baker (Chicago: University of Chicago Press, 2006), 152-9; for a reading of the poem, see Baker, *The Subject of Desire: Petrarchan Poetics and the Female Voice in Louise Labé* (West Lafayette, IN: Purdue University Press, 1996), 93-107.

2   All parenthetical citations are from Madeleine de Scudéry, *The Story*

writer. Both DeJean and Newman, in assessing Scudéry's Sapphic inspiration, assume it announces her identification with the most famous woman writer of antiquity. For both of them, what remains in question is whether or how one could say that Scudéry conveys "l'Amour Lesbienne." That is my question as well.

One reason to doubt that she does is the fact that Sapho's love in Scudéry's fiction is directed at a man, Phaon, the lover who abandons her in Ovid's *Heroides*, a central text that conveys the image of Sappho driven to suicide at his loss. Even there, it has to be noted that her love for Phaon is apparently her first heterosexual passion; before that, it was the "girls" of Lesbos who enchanted her and inspired her songs (Ovid cannot help from regarding this as shameful).[3] The conclusion of Scudéry's *Histoire* has Sapho leaving Lesbos, but in the company of Phaon, to begin a life together on the island of Sarmatae; its overarching law is the rule of love that demands absolute fidelity. Ovid's story of abandonment and suicide is explicitly mocked: "rational people did not believe so improbable a tale," Scudéry's narrator declares (135). For DeJean and Newman, the worry is that this happy ending apparently reinforces an entirely heterosexual form of love as "l'Amour Lesbienne."

Both are quick to point out, however, that Sarmatae, ruled by a queen, has associations with the Amazons that go back to Herodotus. Even more important for them is the fact that Sapho and Phaon's relationship is not a marriage, the institutionalized social form of regulatory heterosexuality. Early in the *Histoire*, when Amithone, one of the four Lesbian women who are Sapho's constant companions, marries, Sapho declares her antipathy to the institution: "I consider it as unending slavery" (19), she explains, declaring, "I will never lose my liberty" (20). At the end of the tale, Phaon petitions the court of Sarmatae to be allowed to marry Sapho; she convinces them instead that for

---

of Sapho, translated by Karen Newman (Chicago: University of Chicago Press, 2003).

3   Ovid, *Heroides and Amores,* translated by Grant Showerman (London: William Heinemann, 1921); see, e.g., *Heroides* xv.19, "quas non sine crimine amavi," for the first such remark (182).

love to last forever, which is what the law of the land demands, "one must never marry" (136). This claim could indeed be an example of the love that animates Sappho's poetry, if we follow the lead provided by Anne Carson's analysis of sapphic love as a striving for a relationality that breaks through conventional limitations. Scudéry seeks in her *Histoire* to refuse normative prescriptions for women that aim towards their subordination in marriage and that equip them for that destiny in an education devoted to making themselves objects of male delectation. Sapho, who declares she wants friends, not lovers, or wants a lover that is also a friend, wants to "to love innocently" (49). "Marital love," she explains to Cydnon, her favorite of her four constant companions, is not "pure or noble enough" (50) to satisfy her desire. What she wants, it seems, entails no physical contact (there is not a kiss or an embrace in her history); it has no institutional form or location except in the utopian realm of Sarmatae. There, eternal union is celebrated by no public rite or bond, although it is the law. "I want a lover without wanting a husband" (51), she tells Cydnon; this love is founded on the belief that "you are loved as much as you love" (51), a mutuality that has no visible sign or proof.

Sapho does not want to be enslaved. Recoiling at Amithone's marriage, she declares, "I am resolved never to let my slave become my tyrant" (20). When Phaon, who has been unfaithful to Sapho, agrees to elope with her to Sarmatae, where he will never part from her, never be out of her company, and where he will seek no other pleasure than her company, he declares this fulfills his desire — to remain her "slave" (131). It could appear that nothing more than a reversal is involved in the plot solution that Scudéry offers. However, from its opening sentences, it is clear that more than reversal is the principal of her story. When the island of Lesbos is first described, it is said to be "so large that in many places you can imagine yourself on the mainland, but...not so mountainous that you think it is nothing but a mass of cliffs rising from the sea, nor...so flat that it offers no heights" (13). The point of this "variety" is to unsettle categories and singularities, locations and limits. We could compare this initial gesture to what Newman takes to be the clinching evidence that the sapphic love of the *Histoire* cannot be contained by its seemingly heterosexual plot. Sapho's poetry is central. Hearing a poem of hers read, Phaon believes that the passion it conveys proves that Sapho had a lover before they met, and perhaps still has one. "The text is careful to make clear that these poems predate Sapho's meeting with Phaon and thus cannot be attributed to her love for him," Newman writes (8), continuing: "In other words, Scudéry writes the love of women for women into her text through the intensity of Phaon's jealousy and suffering," producing what Newman terms "a certain slippage or ambiguity around desire" (9). Indeed. In a kind of proto-Proustian configuration, Phaon's belief in a rival discloses that Sapho's passion for her women friends cannot be distinguished from the love he desires, or from the love, perhaps, that he feels for Sapho (it is so heightened that he is content for it to remain unconsummated, something not the case with his former Sicilian mistress to whom he returns after he and Sapho initially enter into their mutual, innocent love relationship).

This love continues when Phaon steals a poem of Sapho's — it is the only poem of hers quoted in the text of the *Histoire* (on 76). This poem was actually written to Phaon, for him or about him, though withheld, hidden from him. At the point in the text where he would be named there is instead a blank space. Metrically, his name would fit it (indeed, his is the only man's name in the text that would fit), yet it never occurs to Phaon that he is the poem's addressee. So, mistaking the address, assuming it is for a rival lover, he becomes, in effect, his own rival, as Cydnon notes (85), as Sapho does as well (87). Knowledge of the addressee has to be kept secret because it is the nature of Saphic love in the *Histoire de Sapho* that it go unsaid. If Phaon were a good reader, were he the lover who fit Sapho's desire, he would know how to fill in the blank (Sapho's education of Phaon trains him with this goal in mind). As Sapho declares to Cydnon, Phaon should "understand that the verses were either written for no one in particular or were written for him" (87). These two possibilities are versions of the same thing. To be her lover, he must correspond to her desire. Sapho's poems take the form of "your name here" if you can desire what she desires.

In Scudéry's *Histoire de Sapho*, Democedes is Scudéry's narrator; he is the brother of Cydnon. She knows as much about

Sapho as Sapho will tell; she is his source for much of the tale Democedes tells when it involves his absence from Sapho's company. His attendance on her, it needs to be noted, is almost as constant as that of her four female friends—including the friend who is married; her marriage does not seem to preclude her constant attendance on Sapho. Nor is Democedes' gender some bar to being part of her inner circle, nor does it preclude his serving as Scudéry's narrator, her proxy. It is Democedes who first answers Phaon's jealousy, explaining the source of the passion in her poems this way: "[W]hat enabled her to write so tenderly was her naturally passionate soul" (73). "I write tenderly because by nature I have a tender soul," Sapho affirms to Phaon many pages later (89).

As a writer, Sapho is to be found in words written by her soul. Decipherment of sapphic desire locates it in the noplace, the utopia called Sarmatae in which innocent love can last forever. Early in their relationship, Sapho enjoins Phaon not to declare his love for her; it turns out that "he knew very well the art of speaking of love without speaking it" (64). This, too, is Sapho's art, one in which she must always keep herself hidden. "I want to unSapho myself" (31), Sapho declares: she wishes to be done with her public role as marvelous paragon. Rather, she prefers to hold conversations in which she is spoken to "as if" she were not a writer (30). She keeps her writing secret. Even when it is read, it has a blank space for the reader. When Sapho and Phaon declare their mutual love, they exchange "their secret thoughts": "They shared all their thoughts, they understood one another without words" (90). The exchange occurs through their eyes. This is how their love abides: "Phaon was as attentive and assiduous as if he had still to conquer the heart he possessed and Sapho was as correct, as unfailingly sociable and serene, as if his conquest of her were not already complete and certain" (92). These "as ifs" are what is achieved on Sarmatae, when, as if married and joined in bodily union, they remain in that place of self-negation. That place is epitomized by Sapho's eyes; they emit "penetrating fire" and "passionate softness" at once; they are both black and white, like a text whose words say what the blank space says. In them, in her eyes, in her words, are "certain qualities rarely found together" (15).

What are these qualities? As Newman points out numerous times in the notes accompanying her translation, all its key terms — *civilité, gallanterie, esprit* — are incapable of translation; they bring together a "variety" of valences that tend in opposite directions. What they betoken is a certain *je ne sais quoi* that Newman leaves untranslated, a sign of the inability of words to tell the sapphic truth of this *histoire*. It is a truth Scudéry derived from Castiglione's *Book of the Courtier* about the art that must not be shown (to translate "il cortigiano" into the feminine is not to praise a woman, while adjectivally "cortigiana" castigates male courting as feminine wiles). In the circle of Sapho, it is imperative for a woman "to hide her wit cleverly, not display it tastelessly" (45). "There is nothing more troublesome than to be a *bel esprit*, or at any rate, to be treated as if one were" (24). "As if" one were not is how one is to be. "Conversation ought to appear so free and easy that it seems as if you are not holding back your thoughts" (58). As if.

* * *

Karen Newman dedicated her translation of Scudéry to me, "with whom," she puts it, "I have long exercised the art of conversation that is so much the subject of the *Histoire de Sapho*. That Sapho's history is about the friendship between men and women, between men, between women, makes this dedication all the more fitting" (x). Fitting because men are not women, women not men, but what is "between" is perhaps nonetheless the same. As in Sapho's "history," which also, in French, as a *histoire*, is a fiction. A true story that is at the same time an "as if."

6

Chance Meetings

"A Chance Meeting" is the title of the first of the "sketches" in *Not Under Forty*, as Willa Cather referred in the Prefatory Note to the pieces she gathered together in her 1936 collection; "sketches" also is how she characterized Sarah Orne Jewett's writing.[1] I will be discussing Cather's story of an unexpected encounter — "It happened at Aix-les Bains," it opens (3) — and its relation to aesthetic theories offered in that volume, but I also want to stage my own chance meeting of her "Chance Meeting" with "Old Mrs. Harris," the central story of the three gathered in *Obscure Destinies* (1932), the last volume of her stories published in Cather's lifetime.[2] Melissa Homestead, as part of her ongoing project to show how fully collaborative Cather's writing practices were with her partner Edith Lewis (they lived together from 1908 until Cather's death in 1947, and lie buried beside each other in Jaffrey, NH).[3] Working from extant manuscripts, Homestead details substantive changes made by both Cather

---

1 Parenthetical citations are from Willa Cather, *Not Under Forty* (Lincoln: University of Nebraska Press, 1988), v, 77, 89.
2 Parenthetical citations are from Willa Cather, *Obscure Destinies* (New York: Vintage, 1974).
3 See Melissa Homestead, "Willa Cather, Edith Lewis, and Collaboration: The Southwestern Novels of the 1920s and Beyond," *Studies in the Novel* 45, no. 3, Special Issue: The Work of Willa Cather: Creation, Design, and Reception (Fall 2013): 408–41, and "The Composing, Editing, and Publication of Willa Cather's *Obscure Destinies* Stories," which I will be citing from the online *Scholarly Editing: The Annual of the Association for Documentary Editing* 38 (2017), http://scholarlyediting.org/2017/essays/essay.homestead.html.

and Lewis. In some cases, sentences that seem quintessentially Cather can be shown to have been the result of emendations made by Lewis. In a 2017 essay, Homestead examines the manuscript of "Old Mrs. Harris" that Cather sent to her publisher. Its final page is reproduced in Homestead's article; it shows that "Old Mrs. Harris" originally ended with what is now its penultimate sentence, supposedly the thought shared by the two Victorias of Cather's story, mother and daughter (Mrs. Templeton and Vickie), as they will come to look back on the death of Mrs. Harris, their mother and grandmother respectively. "I was heartless because I was young, and so strong, and because I wanted things so much," it read. The final sentence that follows this one in the published text, "But now I know" (190), was added, Homestead imagines, only when Cather and Lewis were reading proofs. Lewis characteristically read them aloud; Cather, Homestead supposes, hearing the original last words, wrote the new final sentence to register her own relationship to the story: it is based on her own family (Victoria stands for her mother Virginia, Vickie for herself). Cather's mother had just died, and now she knew what she had not known at the time.

Also found on the last page that Homestead reproduces is a change made in Cather's hand. Originally, after the story's final words, Cather had indicated where and when it had been written. "Aix-les-Bains, 1930" has been crossed out; below it, Cather wrote "New Brunswick, 1931." That date registers that Cather now knew about the death of her mother on August 31, 1931, news of which reached her on Grand Manan. The original date and place points to the coincidence, the chance meeting I pursue here. Cather was writing "Old Mrs. Harris" at the time of her encounter with Flaubert's niece, the meeting recorded in the sketch that opens *Not Under Forty*. No mention that she was writing "Old Mrs. Harris" occurs there, although Cather's first conversation with Mme Grout (before she knows her name or who she is) does take place when she goes to write, "to write letters" (6), only to find the "old lady" there too. Cather had been eyeing her, "her fine head, so well set upon her shoulders and beautiful in shape, recalling some of the portrait busts of Roman ladies" (4); "the old lady was always impressive," we are told likewise of Mrs. Harris, "Perhaps it was the way she held her head, — so simply, unprotesting and unprotected" (81).

Mme Grout returns Cather's gaze. They start talking — in English — about music, until the French woman interrupts the conversation to ask about a word she has just used, she fears, incorrectly: "[I]t is almost September, the days are lowering now" (8), she had said. Cather remarks that although "growing shorter" would be more idiomatic, "lowering" is "a very good word." "'Mais un peut poétique, n'est-ce pas?' 'Perhaps; but it is the right kind of poetic'" (8). It sounds, Cather explains, like a usage that she had heard among "old-fashioned farmers" in the US, in the South, Cather's place of birth, as well as that of the Harris/Templeton clan in "Old Mrs. Harris." Cather records her satisfaction in the old Frenchwoman's "special feeling for language" (10), or, to be more precise, she tells her reaction to the "friend" with whom she is traveling, the unnamed Edith Lewis. Some days later, still not knowing with whom she had been speaking, she and her friend return to the "writing room." Mme Grout is there again, and from remarks she makes, Cather realizes that she is "the 'Caro' of Flaubert's *Lettres à sa Nièce Caroline*" (15–6). From that moment to the end of the sketch, the conversation of the two women is almost entirely about writing.

After talking one evening, Cather wanders out into the moonlight: "[T]he full moon (like the moon in *Salammbô*) stood over the little square and flooded the gardens and quiet streets and the misty mountains with light" (23); *Salammbô* was Cather's favorite Flaubert novel. "The old lady had brought that great period of French letters very near" (23), so near that Flaubert's moon fills the sky. As the story moves to its close, Mme Grout wants Cather to have one of her uncle's letters, but Cather demurs: "the things of her uncle that were valuable to me I already had" (33); indeed, his niece has them too: "It was the Flaubert in her mind and heart that was to give me a beautiful memory" (33). That is what they share. So, when an envelope containing a letter of Flaubert's to George Sand that Mme Grout sends Cather is pilfered in the mail, Cather claims to have no regrets at its loss. In the interval in her sketch between her last glimpse of the niece and the news of her death that ends the story after the misarrival of the purloined letter, Cather reads again Flaubert's letters to his niece, finding that "the personality of Madame Grout sent a wonderful glow over the pages" (35); Cather reports that she feels as if she might be reading her own family chronicle, finding it especially moving that Flaubert had taken in his niece, the daughter of the sister he "had devotedly loved" (36), making her part of a new family composed of Flaubert and his "old mother" with whom he lived (37).

* * *

In "Old Mrs. Harris," one plot point involves granddaughter Vickie's desire to go to college, something unheard of among the women in the family. The question is discussed by her mother, her grandmother, and Mrs. Rosen, the German-Jewish next-door neighbor; the Rosen home, filled with books and pictures, was "the nearest thing to an art gallery and a museum that the Templetons had ever seen" (103); a library, too, as Vickie borrows books from the Rosens, including *Wilhelm Meister,* Goethe's artist's bildungsroman. Mrs. Harris wonders if Vickie's desire for an education means she has fallen for a young professor with whom her granddaughter had spent some time when he and his students had been on a dig; it was from them that she had learned about a scholarship for women students at the University of Michigan. Victoria pooh-poohs this explanation: "There ain't a particle of romance in Vickie" (150; romance of the Southern belle type is Victoria's essence, although it has led her to marriage and a house full of children, one more on the way as the story ends, ruining the life she wants to lead, and which her mother encourages, taking over much of the housekeeping to help Victoria sustain her romantic illusions). Mrs. Rosen objects: "But there are several kinds of romance, Mrs. Templeton. She may not have your kind" (150). Mrs. Harris agrees, setting the stage for the ensuing plot, in which she helps Vickie attain her desire for a college education.

The romance of letters in "A Chance Meeting" is played out in "Old Mrs. Harris" once Vickie gets a letter of acceptance and offer of a scholarship from Michigan. Taking the unopened letter "from the box, such a wave of fright and weakness went through her that she could scarcely get out of the post-office"

(155). Hiding the letter, she heads to a neighbor's backyard, to "her hammock, where she always felt not on earth, yet of it." She lands there "without seeing anything or knowing what road she took" (155). One might be reading Sappho's Fragment 31 with its similar conflicting feelings to those felt in this place just slightly suspended above the ground and yet offering Vickie something more than earthly experience. She lies in her hammock with her finger throbbing; she has a cut infected with ink. "It was a kind of comfort to feel that finger throb; it was companionship, made her case more complete" (155). Her case? The bittersweet love in writing.

* * *

In a groundbreaking 1984 essay, and in the 1987 biography of Cather that followed it, Sharon O'Brien was the first to make the case for how consequential Cather's sexuality was to her writing, even if explicit lesbian relations are not evident in her fiction.[4] Sappho helped O'Brien make her case, noting, for example, a poem of Cather's, "The Star Dial," that carried the subtitle "A variation upon a theme of Sappho's" when it appeared in *McClure's Magazine* 30, no. 2, in December 1907 (22). This poem was not included when expanded versions of Cather's *April Twilights* (1903) was reprinted in 1923, 1933, and 1937. Fragment 168B lies behind the poem: "Moon has set / and Pleiades: middle / night, the hour goes by, / alone I lie." In Cather's poem, her speaker waits for a lover who never appears as a dawn arises that would, in any case, have necessitated their separation. Theirs is a secret love; although no gender is explicit, the fourth stanza of Cather's light-drenched nocturne is particularly sapphic: "All my pillows hot with turning, / All my weary maids asleep; / Every star in heaven was burning / For the tryst you did not keep." She burns to the end of the poem. O'Brien

4 I refer to Sharon O'Brien, "'The Thing Not Named': Willa Cather as a Lesbian Writer," *Signs: Journal of Women in Culture and Society* 9, no. 4 (Summer 1984): 576–99, https://doi.org/10.1086/494088, and *Willa Cather: The Emerging Voice* (Oxford: Oxford University Press, 1987).

imagines the poem in the context of Cather's affair with Louise Pound years earlier, but perhaps Edith Lewis was its inspiration (they had met in 1903 and were on the verge of living together).

Writing about women poets in the *Nebraska State Journal* in January 1895, her last semester in college, Cather concludes that "there is one poet whom all the world calls great."[5] It is Sappho. "Those broken fragments have burned themselves into the consciousness of the world," she continues: "If of all the lost richness we could have one master restored to us, one of all the philosophers and poets, the choice of the world would be for the lost nine books of Sappho," this, despite the fact that her only subject was love — otherwise "she was unlearned" (1:147). Cather's conclusion somewhat undercuts her praise and echoes with the estimation of women's talents she offers on the previous page (as if she were not one): "A woman has only one gift... to feel greatly." Love therefore would seem to be her only possible subject. But were we to follow Anne Carson's prompting in *Eros the Bittersweet*, we would recall that love and the love of wisdom are akin. This is the direction of Vickie's (Cather's too), intimated when her youthful piece of journalism concludes by extolling where Sappho's understanding of love lead: to the invention of "the most wonderfully emotional meter in literature, the sapphic meter with its three full, resonant lines, and then that short, sharp one that comes in like a gasp when feeling flows too swift for speech." The unsaid says what otherwise cannot be said.

Sappho figures in two letters Cather wrote when she was more or less the age of her alter ego Vickie. However, it is a French Sapho in question there, Alphonse Daudet's novel that attaches the name to a courtesan with a lesbian past who winds up a whore with a heart of gold. Writing to her friend Mariel Gere the summer before she entered college at Nebraska, Cather asks her "what power on earth, or rather under it, tempted you to purchase that abominible [sic] Sappho! I had fallen into that trap myself once, — the name of the book is both innocent and

---

5   I cite Cather's journalism from *The World and the Parish: Willa Cather's Articles and Reviews, 1893–1902*, edited by William M. Curtin, 2 volumes (Lincoln: University of Nebraska Press, 1970), 1:147.

classic — and honestly wished to save you the pain which it gave me. So you see you thwarted the one Christian effort of my life."[6] The joking tone belies the literal. Five years later, in a letter to a group of college friends, including Gere, she asks a favor of her; will Mariel retrieve her copy of Daudet's *Sapho* that she had loaned to a girlfriend with whom she is on the outs? She professes to be "very fond" of the novel as well as its illustrations (25). In 1900, Cather saw a staged version of "Alphonse Daudet's greatest novel," as she terms it in the review she wrote for the *Pittsburg Leader* (2:688). She admired Olga Nethersole's performance of "the glories, the horrible beauty of Sapho...this character involves shades and semitones and complex motives, the struggling birth of things and burnt-out ghosts of things that it baffles psychology to name" (2:688).

Once again, by way of Sappho, or rather, *Sapho*, Cather glances at the kind of feeling she enunciated as her goal in "The Novel Démeublée": "without being specifically named...the inexplicable presence of the thing not named" (*Not Under Forty*, 50). Flaubert and his avatars are models of this for Cather, Jewett among them, as can be seen in "Miss Jewett" in *Not Under Forty*; it opens with a citation from one of her letters remarkably like Cather's own statement of artistic purpose: "*The thing that teases the mind over and over for years, and at last gets itself put down rightly on paper — whether little or great, it belongs to Literature*" (76). Cather praises Jewett's slight writing for the same qualities she found in Flaubert's niece's mot juste ("lowering"). What Jewett calls "Literature" Cather pronounces in her "sketches" to be "not stories at all, but life itself" (78). In the final essay in *Not Under Forty*, on Katherine Mansfield's exploration of the "double life," Cather hails her ability to convey the secret life that lies beneath the "group life" of family and normative sociality, "the real life that stamps the face and gives character to the voices of our friends" (136). Plumbing that real life, "the very letters on the page come alive" (137). Mrs. Rosen seeks this when she tries to catch Mrs. Harris alone, "the real grandmother" (83). She enacts Cather's writerly ambition. Her

6 I cite from *The Selected Letters of Willa Cather*, edited by Andrew Jewell and Janis Stout (New York: Knopf, 2013), 13-4.

name opens "Old Mrs. Harris." "Mrs. David Rosen," her point-of-view, her attempt to know the old woman, to further Vickie's other form of love, coincide with the writer's point of view without being absolutely identical to it. Not a member of the family, not southern, not Christian, she is a neighbor, a friend.

* * *

In September 1932, shortly after "Old Mrs. Harris" appeared in *Obscure Destinies*, it was reprinted in *Ladies Home Journal* as "Three Women." To which group of characters does this title refer, the family group of Mrs. Harris, Victoria Templeton, and Vickie? Perhaps, although Vickie is only on the verge of womanhood. Might the third woman be "Mandy, the bound girl they had brought with them from the South" (88)? ("Girl" she may be called, but she is an adult.) She is attuned to Mrs. Harris, unlike either her self-absorbed daughter or granddaughter. She notices that she is short of breath, the sign in the previous story, "Neighbour Rosicky," and here too, of impending death. Twice, she kneels before Mrs. Harris and rubs her feet, the second time too late to bring back the life leaving her. Self-abnegating Mrs. Harris does not ask "for this greatest solace of the day: it was something that Mandy gave who had nothing else to give" (93). Or is the third woman Mrs. Rosen? Mrs. Harris, who knows how much Mrs. Rosen admires her, turns to her when Vickie's father refuses to supply the $300 she needs to be able to go to college; Mrs. Rosen promises her that her husband will find the money for Vickie. Mrs. Harris weeps: "Thank you, ma'am. I wouldn't have turned to nobody else." "That means I am an old friend already, doesn't it, Grandma," Mrs. Rosen replies. "And that's what I want to be. I am very jealous where Grandma Harris is concerned!" (170). "Friend" is the word Cather has here and for the title of the final story in *Obscure Destinies*, "Two Friends," to name the bond that can create alternate forms of sociality. (Cather uses "friend" for the Boston marriage of Jewett and Mrs. Field, as well as for their literary relations in the two sketches in the center of *Not Under Forty*.) This scene between Mrs. Harris and Mrs. Rosen ends with Mrs. Rosen "lightly kissing...the back of the purple-veined hand she had been holding" (170).

When Willa Cather learns the identity of the old lady in Aix-les-Bains, seeing in her "most of [her] mental past" standing before her, there is "no word" for "such a revelation. I took one of her lovely hands and kissed it, in homage to a great period, to the names that made her voice tremble" (16).

Cather wrote a poem about Marjorie Anderson, the servant who had accompanied her family when they moved from Virginia to Nebraska, upon whom Mandy is based. "Poor Marty," first published in 1931 and included in the later printings of *April Twilights*, ends when the speaker of the poem (an imaginary male servant) imagines the old woman about to enter paradise, hoping that, too, will be his destination; he pays tribute to "Hands that never gathered aught,/But in faithful service wrought."

* * *

Vickie has her most memorable conversation about her form of romance with Mr. Rosen:

> "Why do you want to go to college, Vickie? He asked playfully.
> "To learn," she said with surprise.
> "But what do you want to learn? What do you want to do with it?"
> "I don't know. Nothing, I guess."
> "Then what do you want it for?"
> "I don't know. I just want it." (158)

Wanting it is all that matters: "[I]f you want it without any purpose at all, you will not be disappointed," Mr. Rosen comments on the Kantian aesthetic life he, too, lives, though he also runs a profitable business. He continues the conversation in French. "Le but n'est rien; le chemin c'est tout." James Woodress comments on this moment, claiming this as a favorite sentence of Cather's. It is alluded to in *Not Above Forty*, in the piece on Thomas Mann, the odd-man-out in that volume, about his novel about Joseph and his "shepherd people" (the Jews; they are akin to Jewett's coastal inhabitants or to the farmers that Cather heard in Mme Grout's language and depicted in her western novels and the three late stories joined in *Obscure Destinies*): "A shepherd people is not driving toward anything. With them, truly, as Michelet said of quite another form of journeying, the end is nothing, the road is all. In fact, the road and the end are literally one" (99).

My Google search did not yield the quotation as Mr. Rosen recalls it, but something quite close in the *Histoire de France*. There, Michelet is writing about tales of the education of knights in the fifteenth century. Invariably given exacting, austere educations from older women, amalgams of mother-wife and guardian angel, this feminine teaching adds a *je ne sais quoi* to the knight's formation. He learns that everything fades. "Au but, tout s'evanouit; en cela, comme toujours, le but n'est rien, la route est tout."[7]

This road is glimpsed as "Old Mrs. Harris" closes; it is where Victoria and Vickie will find themselves. "Thus Mrs. Harris slipped out of the Templetons' story; but Victoria and Vickie had still to go on, to follow the long road that leads through things unguessed and unforeseeable" (190), the road of chance meetings that are the meaning of life, our obscure destinies. Mrs. Harris vanishes and becomes part of Vickie and Victoria. Their desires and hers coincide—their selfishness, her selflessness—in the purposeful purposelessness of life. In *Eros the Bittersweet*, Carson writes that from Sappho we glean an awareness of "the very structure of human thinking.... That is...we think by projecting sameness upon difference, by drawing things together in a relation or idea while at the same time maintaining the distinctions between them" (171). "The days are lowering now." Mr. Rosen signs J. Michelet to a French sentence Cather made her own. But now I know.

---

7 Jules Michelet, *Ouevres de M. Michelet* (Brussels: Meline, 1840), Volume 3: *Histoire de France*, 567n2.

7

"*Sapho* to *Philaenis*"

The 1990s were the heyday of criticism of Donne's verse epistle.[1] An article or two — or a book chapter — appeared more or less every year. These lie behind the discussion of the "lesbian phallus" that Catherine Bates offers in a chapter on the poem in her 2007 book on English Renaissance poetry; it opens with the stunning assertion that Donne's "is generally acknowledged to be the first unambiguously lesbian love poem in English" (216). Half her discussion walks back this claim, since critics of the 90s were divided between those who thought Donne successfully represented lesbian love and those for whom his overwhelmingly masculinist presence precluded that possibility. Bates finds these opposite takes as identical insofar as both credit Donne's mastery; instead, she offers a dephallicized reading that nonetheless falls into the pattern she decries, since her Donne too exhibits mastery precisely when he "puts himself under erasure" (241). In his dismantling of phallogocentrism, Donne does not practice an "*écriture féminine*"; rather, femininity is inscribed as loss. Bates claims the poem as lesbian for just the reason that other critics dismissed Donne's poem as failing to be lesbian.

---

1 For a guide, see Valerie Traub, "Recent Studies in Homoeroticism," *English Literary Renaissance* 30, no. 2 (March 2000): 284–329, esp. 299–300, https://doi.org/10.1111/j.1475-6757.2000.tb01173.x, as well as the notes to Catherine Bates, *Masculinity, Gender and Identity in the English Renaissance Lyric* (Cambridge: Cambridge University Press, 2007), Chap. 6, "The Lesbian Phallus in *Sapho to Philaenis*," 216–58, discussed below.

Also looking back on 1990s criticism in her 2002 *The Renaissance of Lesbianism in Early Modern England,* Valerie Traub concludes her book by contesting what constitutes an early modern "*lesbian* voice," a "*lesbian* author," and "*lesbian* writing" ("lesbian" is italicized as a reminder of the distance between representation and a reality that remains to be defined).[2] Donne's poem is faulted for a "*homo-normativity*" (342), alongside Katherine Philips' intense poems of female friendship, inspired often by Donne's lyrics, that, Traub claims, continues to shape understanding of lesbian desire; effacing difference in a poetics of sameness, it conveys pernicious political effects. Her critique does not mean, however, that Traub is comfortable with lesbian representations that feature masculinization (as in the classical and early modern tribade with a strap-on or an enlarged clitoris).

Donne's poem certainly figures the relationship between Sapho and Philaenis through a rhetoric of similitude.[3] Philaenis is first imagined as comparable only to herself: "thy right hand, and cheek, and eye, only / Are like thy other hand, and cheek, and eye" (23-4); Sapho depicts her relationship to Philaenis in similar terms: "My two lips, eyes, thighs, differ from thy two, / But so, as thine from one another do" (45-6). One side of Philaenis resembles the other; Sapho's body parts match those of Philaenis. Do these likenesses preclude difference, however? In *Like Andy Warhol,* Jonathan Flatley studies impulses to likeness, likening, and liking that inform Warhol's images, serial likenesses that display the capacity of making like and of liking everything that Flatley sees enlisted towards a queer project that expands the field of resemblance beyond differences and yet without effacing difference.[4] His crucial point is a simple one: likeness is not sameness, identification is not a making identical

---

2 I quote from Valerie Traub, *The Renaissance of Lesbianism in Early Modern England* (Cambridge, UK: Cambridge University Press, 2002), 338.

3 I will be citing the poem from *The Poems of John Donne,* edited by Herbert J.C. Grierson (Oxford: Clarendon Press, 1912).

4 Parenthetical citations are from Jonathan Flatley, *Like Andy Warhol* (Chicago: University of Chicago Press, 2017).

or the production of identity: "When something is *like* something else it means precisely that it is *not the same* as it" (5). If Philaenis's right side really was identical to her left, "right" and "left" would be meaningless terms. If Sapho and Philaenis's bodies were identical to each other's, they no longer would be Sapho and Philaenis. Sapho's phrasing says that: the two differ just as do Philaenis's two eyes, lips, and thighs. They too are two, not one. The sex that is not one does not lack something, as Bates supposes; nor does similitude produce a phallic norm, as Traub claims.

Traub admits, in passing, where her discomfort with similitude could lead: "[O]ne could submit [the texts she examines] to a deconstructive reading which, by elucidating how figures undo their own logic, might transform surface monovocality into a more hermeneutically satisfying polysemy"; she declines this option, claiming that "these poems thematically invite us to concentrate on surfaces, on mirror images, on similitudes" (340). It's the critic doing the insisting. What would happen if we were to read Donne's poem holding in mind William Empson's brilliant aperçu, that even the strongest claims of identity, when two terms are joined to each other by the copula, only work in one direction? "God is love" is not equivalent to "love is God," as Empson notes.[5]

"*Sapho* to *Philaenis*" opens with a question, two questions: "Where is that holy fire, which *Verse* is said / To have? is that inchanting force decai'd?" (1–2). "That holy fire" is singular yet undefined — is it a biblical flame or Sappho burning? Where is it located — in the speaker's passion or its loss? Is it even in her if verse possesses it, or once did? Whose enchanting power is this? Whatever it is, wherever it is to be located, remains unidentified, and the speaker herself is dislocated. That is, if there is such a thing: the relation of Art and Nature is in question in these opening lines, their powers, their creative ability. Forms of the word "work" appear three times in two lines, meaning something different each time in a sentence that begins and ends with the word "draw" that means at once to depict and to pull away,

5 See William Empson, *Some Versions of Pastoral* (1935; reprinted London: Chatto & Windus, 1950), 143.

drawing in two different directions: "*Verse* that draws *Natures* workes, from *Natures* law,/Thee, her best worke, to her worke cannot draw" (3-4). The speaker herself is similarly divided: her tears may have put out her poetic flame, but they have not quenched her natural desire. Divided between mind and body, her memory works against itself: "*Memory,*/Which, both to keepe, and lose, grieves equally" (12-3). Opposites (keep and lose) equate. She and her beloved are alike apart together: "My fires have driven, thine have drawne it hence" (11) in a nowhere here on the page, in these lines.

The fire in these lines could be sapphic, the burning in Fragment 31 in which the lover is close to dead and yet alive, or in Fragment 38 that reads in Anne Carson's translation "you burn me," or in Fragment 48 ("you came and I was crazy for you/and you cooled my mind that burned with longing"), the epigraph that opens Page duBois' *Sappho is Burning*. In Donne's poem "*Griefe* discolors me./And yet I grieve the lesse, least *Griefe* remove/My beauty" (28-30). "Lesse, least": the echo of the same keeps by losing more.

This fire might be Virgilian. In the song sung by Alphesiboeus in the eighth eclogue, hoping by it to enchant his beloved Daphnis to return to him, he makes an image that melts like wax and blazes. "Onely thine image, in my heart doth fit,/But that is waxe, and fires environ it," Donne's Sapho says (9-10). Onely, only, singly. In Virgil, when the wax simulacrum burns, Daphnis appears. Or is it not Daphnis but an image, a phantasm of the poet's mind that is seen? Sapho looking in the mirror, seeing herself, seeing Philaenis as herself, sees her "loving madnesse" (57). Imaginary identification. Likeness.

Virgilian male same-sex desire resonates in Donne's lesbian poem; male–male desire in his verse letters to R.W. is imagined as the commingling of their female muses. Does cross-gender identification only further male same-sex desire? In "*Sapho to Philaenis,*" as Lynn Maxwell has shown, it is just when the question of comparison becomes explicit that the microcosm/macrocosm trope that is used often in the *Songs and Sonets* to assert male power (more often than not hollowly) and sexual difference appears: "if we justly call each silly *man*/A *little world,*

What shall we call thee than?" (19–20).⁶ The negations that follow might seem to debase Phileanis, "Thou art not soft, and cleare, and strait, and faire, / As *Down,* as *Stars, Cedars,* and *Lillies* are" (21–2), but in refusing to make her fit the analogies, the poem makes her comparable only to herself, an analogy herself. Moreover, it is precisely at this moment, when she is incomparable to anyone but herself, that Sapho makes a comparison — to her previous male lover: "Such was my *Phao* awhile" (25); and to herself: to her idolatrous worshipers "I am such" (28). Where does likeness stop? What does it delimit?

Philaenis is not one of the beloved girls named in any extant fragment of Sappho's. Elizabeth Harvey notes that the names Sappho and Philaenis are coupled in the Pseudo-Lucian's *Amores,* when a male speaker advocates the propriety of female–female love on the model of male–male intercourse: "Let them strap to themselves cunningly contrived instruments of lechery...let our women's chambers emulate Philaenis, disgracing themselves with Sapphic amours."⁷ Harvey builds on a brief note by D.C. Allen that investigated Donne's sources for the name Philaenis and its joining with Sappho.⁸ A tribade in Martial is named Philaenis; she names an author of an ars erotica in the *Greek Anthology.* In fact, the name "Philaenis" appears often in Martial's epigrams, frequently as a byword for an undesirable woman (e.g. 3.33, 4.65, 12.22). Once she is a wife who promises her husband a blowjob when he returns home (9.40). In 7.70, she is said to outtribade tribadery ("Rubber of all

---

6   See Lynn Maxwell, "Woman as World: The Female Microcosm / Macrocosm in Shakespeare and Donne," in *This Distracted Globe: Worldmaking in Early Modern Literature,* edited by Marcie Frank, Jonathan Goldberg, and Karen Newman, 190–211 (New York: Fordham University Press, 2016), esp. 190–1, 205–7. In *Wanton Words: Rhetoric and Sexuality in English Renaissance Drama* (Toronto: University of Toronto Press, 2004), by way of metaphor and metonymy, Madhavi Menon broaches the imbrication of sameness and difference in this poem (38).
7   Elizabeth D. Harvey, *Ventriloquized Voices: Feminist Theory and English Renaissance Texts* (London: Routledge, 1992), 126.
8   See D.C. Allen, "Donne's 'Sappho to Philaenis,'" *English Language Notes* 1, no. 3 (March 1964): 188–91.

girl-rubbers," the Loeb translation opens);[9] all her girl friends are girls she fucks. Epigram 7.67 presents her as a weightlifter who hangs out with gymnasts; she screws boys and performs cunnilingus; only cock-sucking is off bounds for her. She doesn't find it sufficiently virile.

When critics take Donne's Sapho's comparisons literally, they ignore the resonances her lover's name may carry. Once Sapho compares Philaenis to Phaon, she imagines her making love to "some soft boy" (31), something Philaenis does in Martial 7.67 ("Philaenis the bulldyke buggers boys," the poem begins in Gillian Spraggs's online translation),[10] and warns her against submitting to "the tillage of a harsh rough man" (38); this seems unlikely given her literary past; or maybe not. In the epitaph she speaks in the *Greek Anthology,* she claims she has been misidentified as the author of a book offensive to women for its sexual content (7.450; cf. 7.345).

* * *

> Thy body is a naturall *Paradise,*
> In whose selfe, unmanur'd, all pleasure lies,
> Nor needs *perfection*; why shouldst thou than
> Admit the tillage of a harsh rough man?
> Men leave behinde them that which their sin showes,
> And are as theeves trac'd, which rob when it snowes.
> But of our dallyance no more signes there are,
> Then *fishes* leave in streames, or *Birds* in aire. (35–42)

Defending Philaenis against man-handling, Sapho describes their sexual dalliance as untraceable, natural but not procreative, feminine but not womanly (marriage "perfects" girls and makes them women, man-possessed). Extraordinary in lines that resonate with the placelessness and tracelessness said to

---

9 Martial, *Epigrams,* translated by D.R. Shackleton Bailey, 3 volumes, Loeb Classical Library (Cambridge, MA: Harvard University Press, 1993).

10 Martial, Epigram LXVII, Book VII, translated by Gillian Spraggs, 2006, http://www.gillianspraggs.com/translations/philaenis.html.

prove lesbian invisibility is the fact that these lines seem to be recalled later in the seventeenth century; by Aphra Behn in "To the Fair Clarinda, who made love to me, imagined more than woman," when she imagines their love-making as innocent; in the *Essay of Dramatic Poesy*, as Grierson notes, Donne's figure is "doubtless the source of Dryden's figurative description of Jonson's thefts from the Ancients; 'You track him everywhere in their snow'" (2:91). What do fish leave in water, birds in the air? When does the difference between art and nature become moot? If "strange" unions of those unlike are what procreation mandates, so too "Likenesse begets such strange selfe flatterie / That touching my selfe, all seems done to thee" (51–2). Masturbating, she imagines herself as her, or she imagines herself doing Donne, or "done to thee." "I am another," Donne's poem seems to say; the more alike, the more likeness proliferates: "my *halfe*, my *all*, my *more*" (58). "When thou hast done, thou hast not done, / For I have more." Wishing to be her does not preclude being oneself (no self, no likeness to another). What is more than all?

A string of comparisons ends the poem:

> So may thy cheekes red outweare scarlet dye,
> And their white, whitenesse of the *Galaxy*,
> So may thy mighty, amazing beauty move
> *Envy*' in all *women*, and in all *men, love*,
> And so be *change*, and *sicknesse*, farre from thee,
> As thou by comming neere, keep'st them from me. (59–64)

Coming near, being far, likeness is maintained, the likeness of things and persons — of bodies and images, of persons and worlds — not alike.

8

The Country of the Pointed Firs

Sarah Orne Jewett has been comfortably and entirely located in Carroll Smith-Rosenberg's "female world of love and ritual," a placement confirmed by her more than three decades' long Boston Marriage with Annie Fields.[1] Laurie Shannon, in "The Country of Our Friendship: Jewett's Intimist Art," an essay on which I build, locates Jewett within these erotic parameters and is willing to translate them into a reason to call Jewett "lesbian." She builds her argument on Jewett's trope of "the country of our friendship;" this is the terrain of her love for Alice Meynell that Jewett found had widened after a summer spent reading her poetry. Shannon expands on the erotics of Jewett's *Country of the Pointed Firs* through contextualizations that include Edouard Vuillard's intimist art, Swedenborgian philosophy, and Shaker notions of community. Jewett's work, an exercise in local color and small-scale narrative, I venture, may be understood as a version of pastoral by way of its central assumption as William Empson formulated it: "[T]hat you can say everything about

1 Laurie Shannon, "'The Country of Our Friendship': Jewett's Intimist Art," *American Literature* 71, no. 2 (June 1999): 227–62, refers to Carroll Smith-Rosenberg, "The Female World of Love and Ritual: Relations Between Women in Nineteenth-Century America," *Signs: Journal of Women in Culture and Society* 1, no. 1 (Autumn 1975): 1–29, https://doi.org/10.1086/493203, as well as to Lillian Faderman, *Surpassing the Love of Men: Romantic Friendship and Love between Women from the Renaissance to the Present* (New York: William Morrow, 1981) for Jewett's Boston Marriage. Note 58 countenances calling Jewett "lesbian" on the evidence of her letters to Mrs. Fields.

complex people by a complete consideration of simple people."[2] Willa Cather suggested something like this in "Miss Jewett," in *Not Under Forty*, a sketch derived in part from the preface she wrote for a collection of Jewett's writing she gathered in 1925.[3] Shannon ends her essay with Jewett and Cather's relation; that's where my discussion ends as well. Like her, I aim to widen the framework for understanding Jewett's art; I do so under the name of Sappho. Cather pointed in this direction when she concluded her preface by placing Jewett beside Theocritus, finding in her writing "the beauty for which the Greek writers strove" (11).

Greek allusions are frequent in *The Country of the Pointed Firs*, almost always attached to Mrs. Todd, the narrator's landlady, as she is called early and late (15, 130). (Jewett's nameless "I," identified well into the text as a "young lady" (122), is presumably single; Shannon notes that this couple composed of a "'spinster' and a widow" had to be "biographically resonant" [242].) Mrs. Todd, whose garden's odors "roused a dim sense and remembrance of something in the forgotten past" (14), gathers the herbs needed to minister to needs physical and spiritual. She is called a sibyl at the beginning and again at the end of the book (17, 152), an enchantress with her brews (34), Medea (113, 152); "she might have been Antigone" in her "archaic grief" (49). She is a "caryatide" (34), like the Victory of Samothrace (41). Cather's comparison of Jewett to Greek pastoral was fetched from Jewett: "She might belong to any age, like an idyl of Theocritus" (56).

> I glanced at the resolute, confident face of my companion. Life was very strong in her, as if some force of Nature were personified in this simple-hearted woman and gave her cousinship to the ancient deities. She might have walked the primeval field of Sicily; her strong gingham

---

2 William Empson, *Some Versions of Pastoral* (1935; reprinted London: Chatto & Windus, 1950), 137.

3 I will be citing from Sarah Orne Jewett, *The Country of the Pointed Firs and Other Stories*, Preface by Willa Cather (Garden City, NY: Doubleday and Co., 1954).

> skirts might at that very moment bend the slender stalks of asphodel and be fragrant with trodden thyme, instead of the brown wind-brushed grass of New England and frost-bitten goldenrod. She was a great soul, was Mrs. Todd, and I her humble follower. (137)

This recurrent set of classical allusions climaxes at the Bowden Reunion over which Mrs. Todd's mother, Mrs. Blackett, another widow, reigns, "always the queen" (89):

> We might have been a company of ancient Greeks going to celebrate a victory, or to worship the god of harvests in the grove above. It was strangely moving to see this and to make part of it. The sky, the sea, have watched poor humanity at its rites so long; we were no more a New England family celebrating its own existence and simple progress; we carried the tokens and inheritance of all such households from which this had descended, and were only the latest of our line. We possessed the instincts of a far, forgotten childhood; I found myself thinking that we ought to be carrying green branches and singing as we went. So we came to the thick shaded grove still silent, and were set in our places by the straight trees that swayed together and let sunshine through here and there like a single golden leaf that flickered down, vanishing in the cool shade. (90)

These conjurings of ancient Greek rites and ceremonies celebrating heroic enterprises resonate with Sappho's lyrics; they frequently allude to the Homeric past. Fragment 17, apparently a prayer to Hera for safe arrival on a sea journey, recalls the prayers of the sons of Atreus. Jewett's Maine coast, with its difficult currents, its long-separated seafaring people, some of whom can be visited only at intervals of years, provides a similarly precarious geography. Helen's journey is often on Sappho's mind when she writes about her lovers. Mrs. Todd takes the narrator to visit her mother, sequestered on Green Island, whom she venerates. Sappho invokes her mother and daughter, both apparently named Kleis (Fragments 98, 132).

Mrs. Todd has a brother, William (he lives with their mother); Sappho's world includes a brother. And, of course, her lyrics are filled with gardens, spring flowers, and breezes (Fragment 2), lovers crowned with flowers (94). Its ceremonial centers are the weddings alluded to in numerous fragments (27, 30, 103, 111, 112, 113, 115, 116, 117, 141, 161, 169). William's marriage ends *The Country of the Pointed Firs*.

That country is the country of friendship, of "the undecidability of love and friendship," as Shannon says (242). Each vignette inhabits this territory. Mrs. Todd, always the narrator's landlady and hostess, becomes her friend. When they part, she glances at her "friend's face, and sees a look that touched me to the heart" (158). That look carries her to imagine Mrs. Todd returning home to find "her lodger gone. So we die before our own eyes; so we see some chapters of our lives come to their natural end" (159). These ends coincide with allusions to a time out of time shared by these friends, indeed by all the friends in this text. The narrator entertains Captain Littlepage (he brings with him Milton's happy rural seat as a place in his imagination and memory); "we parted the best of friends," "as if" (the phrase recurs throughout) she "were a fellow shipmaster" (32). She is immediately a friend to Mrs. Blackett (39), to William too despite his shy reticence. With both she communicates heart to heart; without words they know each other's thoughts (52, 117–9). But so too do the men on the dock share a "secret companionship" (102). Male–male; male–female; female–female, living and dead, near and far; these friendly relations end nowhere. Almost all the women in the book are widows, the men widowers, almost all are solitary, yet they form a country without borders. Mr. Tilley, befriended by the narrator, is eight years into mourning his wife; her presence is felt in his housekeeping (107) just as his mother is in his knitting (109).

Becoming "like the best of friends" (111), the narrator enters into these relations. She arrived in Dunnet Landing as a third person from whom an "I" emerges who only belatedly acquires a gender and never has a name. A writer who says of herself "I really did not belong to Dunnet Landing" (21), she ends by returning "to the world in which I feared to find myself a foreigner" (158). This not belonging is a form of a wider belonging, as when Mrs. Morton, who imagines herself a twin to Queen Victoria, gives evidence, the "surprising proof of intimacy" between worlds apart (134) that is typical of "the unchanged shores of the pointed firs" (13) or of any "quiet island in the sea, solidly fixed in the still foundations of the world" (120).

* * *

In a December 13, 1908, letter from Jewett to Cather, she urged the young writer: "[Y]ou must find your own quiet centre of life and write from that to the world that holds offices, and all society...in short, you must write to the human heart, the great consciousness that all humanity goes to make up." I cite the passage as Edith Lewis does in *Willa Cather Living*; Lewis goes on to say, "I am sure Willa Cather never forgot this letter...I think it became a permanent inhabitant of her thoughts."[4]

Jewett's advice is somewhat at odds with what she had written Cather a couple of weeks before, after reading "On the Gulls' Road," a story of Cather's just appearing in *McClure's* (Cather also enclosed "The Enchanted Bluff" in her October 24 letter to Jewett).[5] Confessing how close to Cather she felt reading "On the Gulls' Road," Jewett urged Cather to forgo the "masquerade" of writing as a male persona in this story of the narrator's love for Mrs. Ebbling, a northern European woman whose "father was a doctor" (like Jewett's) and "uncle a skipper" (like Jewett's grandfather) (237). Jewett makes no mention of Cather's story of the Sandtown boys (its narrator is one of the boys), their "romance of the lone red rock and the extinct people" (259) that constitutes the world of the friends in that story. It is arguably a story in which Cather found just what Jewett advised her

---

4 Edith Lewis, *Willa Cather Living: A Personal Record* (1953; reprinted Lincoln: University of Nebraska Press, 2000). Jewett's letters to Cather are found in *Letters of Sarah Orne Jewett,* edited by Annie Fields (Boston, MA: Houghton Mifflin, 1911), 234–5, 245–7, 247–50.

5 Parenthetical citations are from Willa Cather, *24 Stories,* edited by Sharon O'Brien (New York: Meridien, 1988).

to find; indeed, Cather could have had a sense of such possibilities of identification in *The Country of the Pointed Firs*; its world barely depends upon its narrator's tenuous gender, nor is it a place of exclusively female–female relationships, although undoubtedly those lie at the center of the text.

Jewett may have been drawn to "On the Gulls' Road" thanks to a letter of Cather's written from Italy in May 1908. Cather was staying in a hotel on the Gulf of Salerno where Jewett had stayed. "Our hotel" (hers and Isabelle McClung's) is also hers and Jewett's; from the window they look out at "the sea of legend" that "Puvis de Chavannes painted" (111; his misty evocations of Greek pastoral could be adduced as a shared point of ekphrasis). "When I was little I knew a funny old lady in Nebraska who had some water from the Mediterranean corked up in a bottle," Cather tells Jewett (111); Mrs. Ebbling in the story likewise recalls "a curious old woman" in her village who had returned from Italy with "a thin flask of water from the Mediterranean. When I was a little girl she used to show me things and tell me about the South...I suppose the water in her flask was like any other, but it never seemed so to me. It looked so elastic and alive" (237); "this was the way it looked," she tells Jewett, "a color and a remoteness that exists in legends and nowhere else" (111). "The sea before us was the blue of legend, simply; the color that satisfies the soul like sleep" (237).

The water in the bottle figures the domain of the work of art. Its routes also shape Cather's letter to Jewett, which proceeds by describing a ceremony celebrating the delivery of St. Andrew's skull to the Amalfi coast 700 years earlier; she joins in. She then tells Jewett that she is reading the essays by Alice Meynell that Jewett had recommended ("how beautifully truthful she is about this pale-colored lovely earth" [112]), and reciprocates by sharing a poem by A.E. Housman with Jewett that "somehow rose out of the limbo of forgotten things and smote me full in the face" (112); she closes by assuring Jewett that her stories "abide with me always" (113).

* * *

In *The Country of the Pointed Firs,* the Greek allusions that surround Mrs. Todd also extend to Esther, the woman who marries Mrs. Todd's brother William after Esther's mother dies; Esther is called a shepherdess. The narrator communes wordlessly with Esther in that inarticulate language of friendship, of things forgotten and recalled in literature's soil. Mrs. Todd describes William as "kind of poetical" (113). "Poetical" echoes a text by another William: "Truly, I would the gods had made thee poetical," Touchstone says to Audrey, beloved by the rustic William, in *As You Like It* (3.3.12). The tongue-tied William is replaced by a courtly clown; his desire for the poetical "implies," as Empson notes about this exchange, "that the most refined desires are inherent in the plainest" (138). The name "William" had to have had a special appeal to Cather; it was how she named herself when young. To the end of her life, she signed herself "Willie" in letters to her beloved brother Roscoe, to old friends like Irene Miner Weisz and Carrie Miner Sherwood, to her nieces Helen Louise, Virginia, Margaret, and Elizabeth, and finally to Roscoe's widow Meta.

9

Carol

Carol is the title given to British editions of Patricia Highsmith's *The Price of Salt* (1952) and to the 2015 film based on Highsmith's novel, directed by Todd Haynes, with a screenplay by Phyllis Nagy.[1] I speculated about the conjunction of Highsmith and Haynes in my book about melodrama.[2] There, I had located Haynes in a genealogy that includes Douglas Sirk and Rainer Werner Fassbinder; Highsmith I treated beside Hitchcock (*Strangers on a Train* being the starting point), and with Cather. These two groupings correspond to two ways of thinking about melodrama — as a plot situation of impossible human relations (impasses of race, class, gender, and sexuality); as the media crossing of word and music that defines melodrama etymologically and formally. In a coda, I proposed a number of alternate routes between and across these two groupings and these authors and filmmakers. At that time, I only could speculate about the meeting of Haynes and Highsmith that was forthcoming in *Carol*, scheduled to open just as I was sending the copyedited manuscript back to the publisher (I first saw *Carol* on Christmas Day, 2015). Based on Cate Blanchett's previous work with Haynes in *I'm Not There* (2007), where she played the only version of Bob Dylan that is a recognizable simulacrum despite the fact that she does not share his gender, I expected Haynes's foray into Highsmith's lesbian novel would further the

1 I parenthetically cite the novel from the 1990 Norton edition that includes Highsmith's 1989 afterword.
2 Jonathan Goldberg, *Melodrama: An Aesthetics of Impossibility* (Durham, NC: Duke University Press, 2016), 164.

queer path he has taken in what he referred to as "my women's films" in his introduction to the screenplays he wrote for *Far From Heaven, Safe,* and *Superstar*.[3]

The Price of Salt, although generically related to lesbian pulp fiction, is neither a coming out story nor a tragic tale of thwarted love. Its final paragraph holds out the possibility of its protagonists being together: Carol has just ended her marriage; Therese, at the beginning of a career as a set designer, also is through with her boyfriend and sometimes bedmate Richard. Therese words the possibility as a stunning fantasy: "It would be Carol, in a thousand cities, a thousand houses, in foreign lands where they would go together, in heaven and in hell" (257). Their future extends into an eternity of Carol, multiplying Carol into the name of all future lovers.

The film offers versions of the novel's final scene twice, at its opening and again at its close. The first time, the camera, at a distance, follows the back of a young man as he enters the bar of a posh hotel and exchanges words with the bartender. As he looks around the room, he sees the back of a young woman whom he recognizes; he approaches her (it is Therese; we see the face of the blond she is sitting with, Carol; he does not know her), interrupting their conversation; he and Therese leave together, heading to a party. In the novel, Therese leaves Carol, too, alone, and with a great deal of ambivalence; Carol has just asked her to move in with her, as she does at the end of the film; she has refused, but also seems to want Carol to realize that no isn't her final answer — "Hadn't Carol heard the indecision in her voice?" (250). In the film, the decision made is accepted by Carol ("That's that," she says in both scripts); its finality is enforced by the young man's intrusion on the scene. He is a stand-in for demands of the world that would keep women from being with each other. In the novel, Therese heads to a party that ushers her into the possibility of a successful career (she will be designing sets for a major play; the well-known actress who will star in it meets her and wants to bed her); in the film, she goes to a party where she knows no one except some people from her

---

3 Todd Haynes, *Far From Heaven; Safe; and Superstar, the Karen Carpenter Story: Three Screenplays* (New York: Grove, 2003), viii.

past, one of whom helped her land a job at *The New York Times* (she is the only woman in her department); her old boyfriend is there, dancing close to some woman; Therese is approached by a woman who knows her old friends; she flees to the bathroom.

The device of opening and closing the film with versions of the same scene derives from *Brief Encounter* (David Lean, 1945), itself based on a play by Noel Coward. Its romantic story of an affair that ends in the adulterous wife's return to her marriage may be a coded gay story; it raises the expectation for an unhappy ending that would signal the impossibility of a future for Therese and Carol. In the novel, Therese hurries from the party back to Carol, out to dinner; when Carol sees her, a smile crosses her face; she raises her arm in a gesture, "a quick, eager greeting Therese had never seen before." The gesture embodies what Therese feels; that she is "a different person" now, where "she" is ambiguously both herself and Carol; they are starting anew: "It was like meeting Carol all over again, but it was still Carol" (257). At the end of the film, the camera follows Therese as she approaches the table where Carol is holding forth to two men and a woman (presumably people from her married life that Therese does not know). The camera holds Therese's face still as she looks, then tracks back from her as she approaches. A smile slowly appears on Carol's face. The music by Carter Burwell that has underscored every moment of their erotic attraction stops abruptly; the screen goes black — a cut that is unlike others in the film. It signals The End. Are there thousands and thousands of possibilities ahead?

* * *

The Price of Salt is an enigmatic title. Salt is cheap, yet without it food lacks savor; it might keep a person alive, but that's all, like the milk Carol gives Therese the first night she stays over at her home: "The milk seemed to taste of bone and blood, of warm flesh, or hair, saltless as chalk yet alive as a growing embryo" (54). Without salt there may be the life a mother gives a child, biological life. Therese wants more. She does not want to be an object, the way she is in her boyfriend Richard's hands; described as "extremely soft, like a girl's, and a little moist," they also are "inarticulate," touching her in the same way "they picked up a salt shaker" (23). After Therese has lost Carol, forever, she supposes, she wonders, "[H]ow would the world come back to life? How would its salt come back?" (233). The thought arises hearing some unidentified tune that she associates with Carol (it could be "Easy Living"): "The music lived, but the world was dead." Salt appears in the text a few pages later. Therese is with Dannie, a physicist (in the film he is a journalist who got her entree to the *Times*). With him she feels "something suspenseful, that she enjoyed. A little salt, she thought" (240). She recalls an earlier moment when he had put his hands on her shoulders: "The memory was a pleasant one"; actually, when it happened "she was uneasy at his touch" (106). The gesture of hand-on-shoulder is an erotic touch in the novel and in the film, as when Carol stands behind Therese at the piano picking out the notes to "Easy Living," and, again, just before they have sex in the motel room in Waterloo; in the novel, the first time Carol holds her that way she kisses her (152); the next time is the novel's Waterloo sex scene.

When Therese sees Carol in the novel for the first time after the divorce, she gives her a present — a candlestick. "It looks like you," Carol says to Therese — of the candlestick. "I thought it looked like you," she answers back (247). Therese looks at Carol's hand handling the gift, "the thumb and the tip of the middle finger resting on the thin rim of the candlestick, as she had seen Carol's fingers on the saucers of coffee cups in Colorado, in Chicago, and places forgotten" (247). "A little salt, she thought. She looked at Dannie's hand on the table, at the strong muscle that bulged below the thumb" (240). When he had touched and kissed her before he had talked about "a kind of right economy of living and of using and using up" (106). These similarities, identities and identifications, these questions about kinds of relations, are central to the novel.

* * *

Joan Schenkar suggests biblical allusions may explain Highsmith's title, thinking it most likely recalls André Gide's *Counterfeiters,* "his novel about the transgressive love of adolescents," as

Schenkar summarizes the plot, going on to quote from Dorothy Bussy's translation: "If the salt have lost its savor wherewith shall it be salted? That is the tragedy with which I am concerned."[4] Gide is probably quoting Matthew 5:13 from the Sermon on the Mount, or perhaps its echo in Luke 14:34. Either way, salt seems to refer to the belief required of would-be disciples. In Mark 9:50 the sentence appears to refer to a way to live that necessitates self-sacrifice. Highsmith's novel glances both ways, to a world that exists only with Carol and to possibilities that might include Dannie. "I don't know what to do/two states of mind in me" (Sappho, Fragment 51). Before she decides to go back to Carol, the novel has Therese's mind "caught at the intersection" of Dannie, Carol, and the actress (256).

Schenkar mentions but does not linger over the most memorable use of salt in the bible, the pillar that Lot's wife becomes when she looks back at the destroyed city of Sodom; her twofold gesture, of departure and retrospective turning back, may be pertinent to the novel, perhaps to the film's structure as well. The biblical allusions come together in St. Augustine's *City of God* (16:30): "Lot's wife stood fixed in the spot where she looked back, and by being turned to salt supplied a bit of seasoning for believers, whereby they may be salted with wisdom to beware of following her example."[5] In 1948, Gore Vidal's novel about gay male desire, *The City and the Pillar,* appeared; its title unmistakably points to Sodom. If Highsmith's title was fetched from Gide or from Vidal, it might signal a connection between her story of lesbian love and the archetypal site for condemnations of male–male sex — and not just in a Judeo-Christian context. "In Islamic legal formulations the crime of sodomy is known as *liwāt* and takes its name from Lot."[6] Lot's wife, the sole member of Lot's family punished for the sins of the city, was not involved in his transgression of

---

4 Joan Schenkar, *The Talented Miss Highsmith: The Secret Life and Serious Art of Patricia Highsmith* (New York: St. Martin's, 2009), 272.

5 Cited in Lowell Gallagher, *Sodomscapes: Hospitality in the Flesh* (New York: Fordham University Press, 2017), 25.

6 I cite from my introduction to *Reclaiming Sodom* (New York: Routledge, 1994), 1–22, at 10.

the laws of hospitality and the untoward sexuality it incited. She becomes the marker of the remembrance of what must be forgotten. She pays the price of salt. Her role raises questions about the relationship of female–female to male–male sexuality also found in the novel.

* * *

A sidenote on Gide's translator, Dorothy Bussy. She was born Dorothy Strachey, sister to Lytton Strachey, Virginia Woolf's best friend and almost husband; a bugger, she called him. Dorothy wrote one novel published under the authorial name of its title, *Olivia* (1949). It is about a girl's love for her French boarding school teacher, Mlle Julie. The novel is dedicated "To the beloved memory of V.W." Dorothy Strachey loved women; she married the French painter Simon Bussy; they had a daughter who became a painter; she loved Gide and translated him into English.

* * *

In an interview with Nick Davis that appeared in *Film Comment*,[7] Todd Haynes comments on how unimaginable and therefore how possible lesbian sex was in the 1950s; two women living together would not raise the suspicions that unmarried male–female roommates would do (male couples, too, presumably). A visual equivalent for this un/imaginable possibility might be the opening shot of the film that appears beneath its titles, abstract filigree that turns out to be the cover in the pavement below which arises the subway noise first heard. The ordinary and extraordinary coincide, the hidden and the visible, the secret and the truth. How does the sex that is not one — lesbian difference — sit beside the Lacanian dictum that there is no sexual relationship?

* * *

[7] Nick Davis, "The Object of Desire," *Film Comment* 51, no. 6 (Nov/Dec 2015): 30–5.

In the novel Carol offers theories about sexual relations. In the long letter she sends Therese after she is compelled to break off their affair, and which is quoted in the fragments Therese reads, a citation that begins in mid-sentence seems to suggest a continuum from their kisses to heterosexual sex, but not without the difference gender makes: "But between the pleasure of a kiss and what a man and woman do in bed seems to me only a gradation.... I wonder do these men grade their pleasure in terms of whether their actions produce a child or not, and do they consider them more pleasant if they do" (229). Gradation, a continuum, becomes grading, scoring a point for reproductive culture. Much earlier in the novel, Carol opines that "people often try to find through sex things that are much easier to find in other ways" (68). By the time her desires are being debated by the lawyers, the value of sexual pleasure cannot be viewed as a substitute for something else. "But the most important point I did not mention and was not thought of by anyone—that the rapport between two men or two women can be absolute and perfect, as it never can be between men and women" (229). Not wanting to compare apples and oranges, she nonetheless does. "The resolution of those contradictory facts was nowhere but in Carol herself, unresolved" (188); so Therese thinks about Carol's reckless behavior, her insisting on continuing their road trip together when they are being tailed by a detective conveying information back to the lawyers. Carol is of two minds. Is Highsmith?

Why does Therese obliquely reveal her feelings about Carol by asking Richard whether he has ever been in love with a boy, qualifying her question by insisting she is not talking about people "like that" but about two people who find themselves in love? The film has an identical scene. Women "like that" are spotted in the film (in the record store where Therese buys Carol her Christmas present, Billie Holliday singing "Easy Living"), and in the novel (Therese thinks of two women she saw in a bar, one with "hair cut like a boy's" [128], a page before she and Carol have sex; she worries that Carol will find her desires disgusting [165]). The novel has a large investment in thinking of Carol as sui generis, and in having Carol think the same thing about Therese; she embraces her as "my little orphan"

(163) although her mother, who abandoned Therese to a Catholic orphanage, is still alive. "What a strange girl you are," Carol says to Therese when they first have lunch, after pondering her strange name — Belivet (believe it; does Highsmith have Ripley in mind?), "[f]lung out of space" (40). She repeats her words when they have sex the first time (the film's script reiterates both exchanges), "My angel... [f]lung out of space" (168).

The sapphic fantasy of the novel is presented in an extraterrestrial world made by the couple; it is explored on their road trip when it leads them to places they hadn't expected to go, where they might spend the night "without pyjamas or toothbrushes, without past or future, and the night became another of those islands in time, suspended somewhere in the heart or in the memory, intact and absolute" (190). It is then that pleasure is absolute, happiness so complete that "it was more often painful than pleasant" (191); "it seemed they flew along in a space, a little closer to heaven than to earth...a certain immeasurable territory of the mind" (191). In the film that other world most often takes place inside a car.

* * *

It is Christmas Day. Therese is in Richard's room. It has a green carpet, just like the room in Carol's house where they sit most often. Carol's car is green, its upholstery is green, green inside and out. Richard gives Therese a skirt trimmed in green and gold. Carol's scarf is green and gold. "Carol was like a secret spreading through her, spreading through this house too, like a light invisible to everyone but her" (78). Richard kisses her: "'Terry, you're an angel,' Richard's deep voice said, and she thought of Carol saying the same thing" (79); she thinks of something Carol will say almost a hundred pages later when they make love. Are lesbians part of the world or apart from it? Outside it or a secret truth? "And she did not have to ask if this was right, no one had to tell her, because this could not have been more right or perfect" (168).

* * *

In the afterword she wrote in 1989 when *The Price of Salt* first appeared under her own name (it had been published under the name of Claire Morgan), Highsmith offers an account of the germ of her story, a concentrated fantasy, elements of which appear dispersed in the novel. Like Therese, she had taken a part time Christmas job as a salesgirl in a department store: "One morning, into this chaos of noise and commerce, there walked a blondish woman in a fur coat." That the woman was "blondish" was one reason she drew Highsmith's attention: "Perhaps I noticed her because she was alone or because a mink coat was a rarity, and because she was blondish and seemed to give off light" (259–60). First described as walking, she is immediately redescribed as having "drifted" into view, becoming disembodied light; distracted, her gaze is hard to reckon, "a look of uncertainty." What is she looking for? What is Highsmith seeing? A vision, the cause of vision: the empirical becomes something else. Is she looking for a doll or for a substitute for it? (The opening encounters with Therese in the novel will play out these possibilities.) The detail that she was, or, rather, that Highsmith recalls her "slapping a pair of gloves," whatever else it suggests, gives off the erotic charge of a dominatrix. In the novel it is summed up in sentences like this: "Carol gave her the derogatory smile that Therese loved" (163). This woman comes from somewhere else — class marks her, but also the fact that she is alone and looks lost, looks as if she is looking for something other than a doll. With her came the story Highsmith invented "as if from nowhere" (260), writing it as soon as she recovered from the flu symptoms that attended her encounter: "I felt odd and swimmy in the head, near to fainting, yet at the same time uplifted, as if I had seen a vision"; "fire is racing under the skin/and in eyes no sight and drumming/fills the ears" (Fragment 31). Cate Blanchett embodies this vision. Love as disease, eros the bittersweet.

This vision posed a problem to Highsmith as a writer: "If I were to write a novel about a lesbian relationship, would I then be labelled a lesbian-book writer?" (261). Lesbians — if that is what Carol and Therese are — rarely do appear in subsequent Highsmith novels; she is best known as the inventor of Tom Ripley, the protagonist in five novels stretching over her career;

in *Plotting and Writing Suspense Fiction*, Highsmith claims that Tom wrote *The Talented Mr. Ripley*: "No book was easier for me to write, and I often had the feeling Ripley was writing it and I was merely typing" (76). Claire Morgan was not her only pseudonym. Sometimes she signed herself "Tom." Did Highsmith ever stop being a lesbian writer? Did Sappho, when she wrote, "I am broken with longing for a boy by slender Aphrodite" (Fragment 102)?

* * *

Richard Brody, writing in *The New Yorker*,[8] reports the experience of seeing *Carol* twice, first from the back of the large auditorium when it premiered at the New York Film Festival, then soon after closeup in a smaller venue. Initially he was taken by images that "didn't so much arouse emotions as signify them." The second time he was taken by the grain of the film, by the film's favored shots that bring it out — the two women behind glass, spattered with rain or snow, glass that reflects light or that reflects themselves back. This camera work is transferred in the film to Therese; she is a budding photojournalist. Haynes and his cinematographer Edward Lachman have claimed inspiration from women photographers of the time of Highsmith's novel, "Ruth Orkin, Ester Bubley, Helen Levitt and Vivian Maier," Lachman lists in a piece in *Indiewire*.[9] "We also looked at Saul Leiter," his "layered compositions that are obscured by abstractions," he continues. These visual effects correspond perhaps to the fantasmatic origin of her novel that Highsmith reports — indeed, of all of her novels, in which she transports herself through characters whose identifications lead them into boundary-crossing perilous territory. The nowhere out of which

---

8 Richard Brody, "'Carol' Up Close," *The New Yorker*, November 30, 2015, https://www.newyorker.com/culture/richard-brody/carol-up-close.

9 "Edward Lachman Shares His Secrets For Shooting Todd Haynes' 'Carol,'" *Indiewire*, December 3, 2015, https://www.indiewire.com/2015/12/edward-lachman-shares-his-secrets-for-shooting-todd-haynes-carol-48627/.

her fictions come is expressed when Therese thinks over and again that what she wants by wanting Carol is to die. Carol is the ordinary name for an extraordinary fantasy; Highsmith played it out in her erotic life, as Schenkar details it: each year another novel; each year, more or less, another lover; each time, she was idolized; each time, the affair lasted as long as it took to write a book. A thousand cities, a thousand houses, is a way to name this pattern.

With Carol, Therese has a nagging sense of déja vu. Sister Alicia, the nun she adored, and who gave her a pair of green gloves, "Sister Alicia in a thousand places, her small blue eyes always finding her out among the other girls, seeing her differently" (5), is an early mentioned precursor of Carol. Before Carol appears, another older woman, Therese's broken-down fellow worker, takes her home, dresses her up like a queen in a fairy tale, and puts her to bed. Therese feels terrified, as if "Mrs Robichek was the hunchbacked keeper of the dungeon" (13). When Carol brings her that warm drink of maternal milk, she swallows it "as people in fairy tales drink the potion that will transform, or the unsuspecting warrior the cup that will kill" (54). Therese keeps passing out from desire; passing out not to desire, becoming again the child of the mother who abandoned her. After Carol also has abandoned her she sees a portrait of a woman identical to one that had hung in her school; its head is "arrogant," its look is "mocking." "It was Carol" (232). Therese tells Carol about the picture that has haunted her. "'Strange,' Carol said quietly. 'And horrifying.' 'It was.' Therese knew Carol understood" (247). Like a magical scene of psychoanalysis, once told, the image dissipates. Carol is not the mother who betrayed her. Rather, she is like the atoms Dannie describes to Therese, fated to swerve and meet: "I think there's a definite reason for every friendship just as there's a reason why certain atoms unite and others don't.... I think friendships are the result of certain needs that can be completely hidden from both people, sometimes hidden forever" (104). For Dannie, these connections point to the fact that "everything's alive" (105); sometimes, he reports, he has had that feeling on horseback, as if "we were a whole tree simply being stirred by the wind in its branches" (106). When he says this, Therese thinks of Sister Alicia and the gloves she gave her and never used, "neither worn nor thrown away" (106).

In the film, figures arise from the grain. Brody treats this conjunction as a warrant for liberal identification: Carol and Therese are two ordinary people falling into a love unjustly condemned. "Theirs is a love that *should* be ordinary," is the message Brody reads in the grain of the film. Perhaps the grain — or the atomic particles — means something else, more like what Leo Bersani makes out of what physicist Lawrence Krauss writes, that "we are all, literally, star children, and our bodies made of stardust." Krauss calls this literality "one of the most poetic facts I know."[10] We are all made of the same stuff. Therese and Carol are made of words and images.

* * *

As Haynes told Davis in *Film Comment*, he worked with Nagy to try to restore to her script the intensity that Highsmith achieved from telling the story entirely from Therese's point of view. Nonetheless, the film gives Carol a life separate from what Therese experiences and sees; Therese with her camera stands in for Haynes. The portfolio she finally assembles are stills from the film. Although Carol has separated from her husband Harge Aird (who erred?) and plans to divorce, as Carol tells Therese over their first lunch together, he still has a key to the house, still can get Carol to go to a party with him. She is shown trapped in their relation, locked into their marriage. Even more, she is tied to their daughter Rindy (in the novel the child is only a voice on the phone or a picture on a mantel; in the film, Carol shows Therese Rindy's picture when she buys her Christmas present; when Therese arrives at Carol's house, Rindy runs out; the Christmas tree that she and Carol buy and trim in the novel instead is trimmed with Rindy while Therese sulks in the kitchen). Carol is a devoted mother; to hold on to her daughter, she is willing to undergo psychiatric treatment and, even more unbearable, since we are shown it, to have dinner with Harge's

10 Quoted in Leo Bersani, *Thoughts and Things* (Chicago: University of Chicago Press, 2015), 77.

parents (Eisenhower on the TV, adding to the chill). We see Carol with her lawyer — it is because Harge is introducing a morality clause that the divorce proceedings have been delayed; that is why Carol takes her road trip with Therese; once things get ugly, she rushes back (in the novel the trip — and the sex — goes on for weeks). Carol gives up right away; she writes to Therese ending their relationship. Finally, she does give up Rindy for her own good. "We're not ugly people," she tells Harge; the film has presented him as an overbearing drunk with a violent temper who only misses hitting Carol because he can't stand up. Carol remains in the film in the social position in which she is first depicted. Therese winds up looking like her when they have tea at the Ritz. The film presents their love as a seduction in style.

The life Nagy gives Carol no doubt reflects social realities, and not just from the 1950s; the novel minimizes what the film maximizes. Carol succinctly reports her dealings with the lawyers: "I refused to make a lot of promises.... I refused to live by a list of silly promises...I didn't promise very much in court, I refused there, too" (248). As Carol announces that she is almost ready to give up Rindy, Therese thinks it's time to get rid of Sister Alicia's gloves. The realism of the film (including a brief for lesbians as good mothers) shortcuts the poetic/literalism that the film achieves in its inspired camera work. As the novel opens, Therese is reading the department store workers' manual, which seems to her like an invitation to a life in prison while she eats the cafeteria food, gray meat swimming in brown gravy. She tries to think of something else: "The great square window across the room looked like a painting by — who was it? Mondrian.... What kind of a set would one make for a play that took place in a department store?" (4). Therese might be looking through Saul Leiter's lens or out Ruth Orkin's window. That other world is where the novel is set in Highsmith's prose, and in Haynes's extraordinary framing and cutting.

10

"To begin with Sappho"

I quote the opening of a letter Virginia Woolf sent to *The New Statesman* responding to an October 2, 1920 piece by Desmond MacCarthy supportive of Arnold Bennett's notion of "women's inferior intellectual power," in the words of the editors of Woolf's diaries, "...in terms which Virginia Woolf found too provocative to ignore" (2:339).[1] Woolf's October 9 rejoinder took up MacCarthy's claim that "no amount of education and liberty of action" could reverse women's innate intellectual inferiority. Woolf insisted on the increasing numbers of "remarkable" English women from the sixteenth through the nineteenth centuries; she ends by scoffing at the impossibility of there ever having been a female Homer by summoning Sappho: "I have been told that Sappho was a woman, and that Plato and Aristotle placed her with Homer and Archilocus among the greatest of their poets" (2:340).

MacCarthy was not convinced. Woolf began again a week later moving on "from Sappho to Ethel Smyth" (2:341) to argue that the social condition of women explains the limits on women's accomplishments, *not* some inherent difference between men and women. Or, if there is, it lies in "the fact...that women from the earliest times to the present day have brought forth the entire population of the universe" (2:341–2); this places them in "subjection to men...and incidentally — if that were to the point — bred in them some of the most lovable and

1 All citations from *The Diary of Virginia Woolf,* edited by Anne Olivier Bell, 5 volumes (New York: Harcourt, 1977–84). Woolf's response is printed as Appendix 3 in 2:339–42.

admirable qualities of the race" (2:342). At one and the same time Woolf couples and decouples women's procreative capacity from virtues "bred in them" by their maternal ability; she ends her letter with the stalemate of "an eternity of domination on the one hand and of servility on the other" (2:342). Intellectual differences cannot be adduced from biology.

Following a prompt from J.A. Symonds, Woolf assumes that it was possible for Sappho to have existed because women on Lesbos had the same educational opportunities as men and were not subjected to male domination. Anticipating *A Room of One's Own,* Woolf opines that there never could have been a female Shakespeare because English women lacked what he had, predecessors of the same gender, male associates, and the "freedom of action and experience" that came thereby. "Perhaps in Lesbos, but never since, have these conditions been the lot of women" (2:341). Ethel Smyth may have had the usual female education that enabled her to sing or play an instrument, but the door was not open for her, nor did her parents welcome her desire to become what she did become, a composer: in the opening decade of the twentieth century, two of her operas were performed at Covent Garden; in 1903 *Der Wald* had two performances at the Metropolitan Opera in New York. It took another century for another opera by a woman, Kaija Saariaho's *L'Amour de Loin,* to be performed there. Plus ça change plus c'est la même chose.

Woolf's letters in *The New Statesman* offer a glimpse of her prescient feminist thought and the milieu in which it was formed — MacCarthy was a lifelong friend, a Cambridge Apostle like Woolf's husband Leonard and closest friends Lytton Strachey and E.M. Forster. Woolf barely mentions her response to his piece in her diary, just a note on October 1 that "Women" is on her list of things to write (2:70); her commiseration with the MacCarthys' financial woes is mentioned a month later (2:74). The Memoir Club, to which Woolf contributed, was founded by Molly MacCarthy, Desmond MacCarthy's wife, in the hope, the diary editors note, "of inducing [him] to write something other than journalism" (2:23n9). He chose the nom de plume "Affable Hawk" for his *New Statesman* column, a sobriquet that perhaps meant to soften his aggressivity, conjuring up thereby the

Figure 2. Virginia Woolf wearing her mother's dress (1924).

possibility of another kind of masculinity than the one Woolf figures in the binarism of male domination and female servility. That alternative is conjured too when Woolf cites Symonds. "To skip from Sappho to Ethel Smyth" is a jump. Woolf met Smyth a decade after she mentioned her in the response to MacCarthy. They became great friends, Woolf basking in "the old fires of Sapphism...blazing for the last time," as she puts it in her diary on June 16, 1930 (3:306). "Ethel yesterday in a state of wonderment at her own genius. 'Can't think how I happened' she says, putting on my hat, & bidding me observe what a nutshell it is on the top of her gigantic brow" (November 23, 1930; 3:334). (See Fig. 2.)

* * *

Woolf's "Sapphism" is my topic in the pages ahead, *Orlando* and *A Room of One's Own* my focus. *Orlando* (1928), of course, is connected to Woolf's affair with Vita Sackville-West. They had met in December 1922; Woolf writes in her diary on December 15, "She is a grenadier; hard; handsome, manly" (2:217). "She is a pronounced Sapphist, & may, thinks Ethel Sands, have an eye on me, old though I am," she notes a couple of months later (February 19, 1923; 2:235). "Sapphist" is attached here to an allegation and rumor; "pronounced" is not exactly "is"; what Sands says (it takes one to know one?), Woolf does not see as possible. It took several more years for Woolf to come to know what she wrote in her diary on December 21, 1925: "These Sapphists *love* women; friendship is never untinged with amorosity" (3:51); by then, she and Vita had had sex. From January 1926 on, their letters are love letters. As late as April 5, 1929, Woolf is asking "Do you love me?" in a letter to Sackville-West in which she reports telling her sister Vanessa Bell about their relationship: "[T]old Nessa the story of our passion in a chemists shop the other day. But do you really like going to bed with women she said — taking her change. And how d'you do it" (no. 2015, 4:36).[2]

Woolf was finishing *To the Lighthouse* when the affair began; she announces the germ of *Orlando* in her diary on March 14, 1927, as the story of "two women, poor, solitary at the top of a house" (3:131). It's not as dreary as it sounds; from their perch everything can be seen, "the Tower Bridge, clouds, aeroplanes" (131). This vantage will become the vista from the oak tree on Orlando's estate.[3] It is to be a fantasy: "The Ladies are to have Constantinople in view" (Orlando will be ambassador there, at just the point in the text where sources about Orlando's affairs with women become fragmentary, sapphic, anticipating his change of sex from male to female[4]). It's to be written at full

2   All parenthetical citations are from *The Letters of Virginia Woolf*, edited by Nigel Nicolson and Joanne Trautmann, 6 volumes (New York: Harcourt, 1975–80). For a detailed chronology of Woolf and Sackville-West's relationship, see Jean O. Love, "*Orlando* and Its Genesis: Venturing and Experimenting in Art, Love, and Sex," in *Virginia Woolf: Revaluation and Continuity: A Collection of Essays*, edited by Ralph Freedman, 189–218 (Berkeley: University of California Press, 1980).

3   Virginia Woolf, *Orlando: A Biography*, edited by Maria DiBattista (New York: Harcourt, 2006), 14–5. All subsequent citations are from this edition.

4   For a succinct consideration of the racial/colonial complexities of the text, see Jaime Hovey, *A Thousand Words: Portraiture, Style, and Queer*

speed, a mix of "satire & wildness"; "My own lyric vein to be satirized. Everything mocked." "Sapphism is to be suggested" (the ladies of Llangollen among Woolf's models).

This sapphic writing project is precisely that; it could as easily bear the title that *A Room of One's Own*, also on Woolf's mind, first bore, "Women and Fiction." Orlando is a writer; by age 25, his oeuvre includes "some forty-seven plays, histories, romances, poems; some in prose, some in verse; some in French, some in Italian; all romantic, and all long" (57). This list spoofs Sackville-West's bibliography. All these works are destroyed in *Orlando* after they are criticized by Nick Greene; hundreds of years later, he recurs in the text to promote publication of "The Oak Tree," the poem Orlando spends the entire novel writing; it is a prizewinner, as was Sackville-West's "The Land." Woolf treats Sackville-West's writing as she does her own, mocking what she nonetheless takes seriously.

Orlando is subtitled *A Biography*. The writer pauses often in the account of Orlando's life to puzzle out the writing problems it involves, the most obvious being the fact that Orlando, a teenager at the time of Elizabeth I, has, as the novel ends on October 11, 1928, recently given birth at age 36 to a son. Further confounding the ordinary temporal parameters of biography is Orlando's change of sex from male to female. "Life? Literature? One to be made into the other?" (209); women and fiction is in question. The biographer, needless to say, identifies as male. Contemplating sixteen-year-old Orlando, he effuses: "Happy the mother who bears, happier still the biographer who records the life of such a one! Never need she vex herself, nor he invoke the help of novelist or poet" (12). "Happy...happier": if only life and literature were such perfect mirrors of each other; yet the similitude, the comparison, points to a difference even as centuries apart are brought together into a single lifespan, even as he and she constitute "such a one." "Green in nature is one thing; green in literature another" (14). One thing, another thing, yet both are still things. "He—for there could be no doubt of his sex," *Orlando* begins, when that is exactly what is in doubt.

Modernism (Columbus: Ohio State University Press, 2006), 77–82.

"Sapphism is to be suggested" thereby; "a pronounced Sapphist" is a mode of articulation, a style of writing and being.

March 6, 1927, Woolf writes to Sackville-West: "I lie in bed making up stories about you" (no. 1726; 3:342). Two days later, she tells her, "I've thought of an entirely new book; it may be two. Each more entirely new than the other" (3:344). (Are the two *Orlando* and *A Room of One's Own*?) October 13, 1927, now writing *Orlando,* she tells Sackville-West, "Orlando will be a little book...I make it up in bed at night...I'm so engulfed in Orlando I can think of nothing else...I think of nothing but you all day long" (no. 1821; 3:430). She writes "as if automatically, on a clear sheet: Orlando: A Biography. No sooner had I done this than my body was flooded with rapture and my brain with ideas" (no. 1820; 3:428). "But listen; suppose Orlando turns out to be Vita; and it is all about you and the lusts of your flesh and the lure of your mind" (3:429). If *Orlando* turns out to *be* Vita, whose mind and body does it record? "Launched somewhat furtively but with all the more passion," Woolf reports herself "in the thick of the greatest rapture known to me" (October 22, 1927; 3:161). "Orlando: Vita; only with a change about from one sex to another. I think, for a treat..." (October 5, 1927; 3:161).

* * *

Sackville-West reports her own version of these sapphic identifications in a letter to Woolf, written after she read the published book, dedicated to her, full of photos of her: "you have invented a new form of Narcissism — I confess, — I am in love with Orlando — this is a complication I had not foreseen."[5]

* * *

In the novel, Orlando's attachment to the ancestral house reflects Sackville-West's Knole, where she was born, and which was no

---

5 *The Letters of Vita Sackville-West to Virginia Woolf,* edited by Louise DeSalvo and Mitchell A. Leaska (New York: William Morrow, 1985), 289. Sackville-West alludes to the permission she gave Woolf a year before to fictionalize her; see 229.

longer hers on her father's death in 1928. Woolf first visited it in July, 1924; her July 5 diary entry gives her mixed impressions; she is resistant to the house, which seems to her lifeless, but she finds its life embodied in Vita: "All these ancestors & centuries, & silver & gold, have bred a perfect body. She is stag like, or racehorse like, save for the face, which pouts, & has no very sharp brain. But as a body hers is perfection" (2:306). "Knole almost crushed me," she writes to Sackville-West the next day, "for I detest being unable to express anything of what I feel, and certainly couldn't" (no. 1484; 2:118). These conflicting reactions to Knole are transformed into the erotic charge of Vita's body. By September 15, she has become more than an example of breeding; Woolf begins to admire Sackville-West's writing. Most to the point, she inspires Woolf's writing: "Vita...is like an over ripe grape in features, moustached, pouting, will be a little heavy; meanwhile, she strides on fine legs,...has a manly good sense.... Oh yes, I like her" (2:313). Orlando has a similar reaction to his first beloved, the Russian Princess Marousha (Masha for short; Violet Trefussis, a former lover of Sackville-West's, as Woolf makes explicit in her diary on October 22, 1927, was her model; 3:162): "Images, metaphors of the most extreme and extravagant twined and twisted in his mind. He called her a melon, a pine apple, an olive tree, an emerald, and a fox in the snow all in the space of three seconds" (28). Orlando's exuberant figurations match Woolf's metaphoricity: Knole provides a resource, a material place ripe for these transformations. In January 1927 she records another visit there: "Vita took me over the 4 acres of building"; they are still not to Woolf's taste, but Vita is, and Orlando comes closer into being: "Vita stalking in her Turkish dress, attended by small boys"; a cart of wood is delivered and Vita explains, "They had brought wood in from the Park to replenish the great fires like this for centuries: & her ancestresses had walked so on the snow with their great dogs bounding by them. All the centuries seemed lit up, the past expressive, articulate; not dumb & forgotten;...& so we reach the days of Elizabeth quite easily" (3:125). Temporal distance is overcome by "a sense of links fished up into the light which are usually submerged," Woolf concludes. What lives in Vita is the other life called *Orlando*. Woolf will term it a reality principle; it is the thing itself at which her writing aims.

That life eludes the biographer intent upon recording facts and necessarily at sea when Orlando starts thinking or writing: "[A]ll these sights, and the garden sounds too, the hammer beating, the wood chopping, began that riot and confusion of the passions and emotion which every good biographer detests" (13). When the novel ends, and "the house was no longer hers entirely.... It belonged to time now; to history; was past the touch and control of the living" (233); that is not exactly the case with the house on the page. "Was not writing poetry a secret transaction, a voice answering a voice?" This secret communication beyond human control and yet a form of living is "the thing itself" (238).

"Itself" also is what Orlando finally becomes, "she was now one and entire" (235). That entirety includes what isn't oneself: "Every thing was partly something else, and each gained an odd moving power from the union of itself and something not itself" (237). That strange animating power is the life on the page: "[W]ith this mixture of truth and falsehood her mind became like a forest in which things moved, lights and shadows changed, and one thing became another" (237). This likening does not turn the forest itself into a figure of speech even as it serves the metaphoricity by which fiction achieves its "itself."

When Orlando had first seen Masha, his worry about this ravishing creature dressed in the "loose tunic and trousers of the Russian fashion" (27) had been his inability to determine its gender: "alas, a boy it must be...Orlando was ready to tear his hair with vexation that the person was of his own sex...legs, hands, carriage, were a boy's, but no boy ever had a mouth like that..." (28). That Masha resolves into a woman is no more a resolution than when Orlando becomes one, and stays one. The truth of gender thereby revealed is that it is not one. Faced with the Victorian imperative to marry, Orlando finds a man who seems to her to be a woman; he finds her a woman who seems to be a man. They make the perfect couple, coupling man and woman: "'You're a woman, Shel!' she cried." "'You're a man, Orlando!' he cried" (184). "'Are you positive you aren't a man?' he would ask anxiously, and she would echo, 'Can it be possible you're not a woman?'" (189). (This couple is based on Sackville-West and her husband Harold Nicolson, at once happily married, each involved in same-sex relations as well.) The truth about time and place embodied in Orlando is a truth about sex and gender. Orlando is no doubt finally a woman, a mother; yet she cannot simply be a woman if "woman" is to be defined solely in relationship to the supposed opposite sex, or in terms of maternal capacity.

Orlando encounters these definitional fictions of sexual difference in the nineteenth century; she sees them manifest in the artifices of crinolines (meant to hide at the same time as to always suggest pregnancy) and wedding bands conferring ownership. Woolf offers her own version of the opening pages of Foucault's *History of Sexuality: An Introduction*. The sexual openness of early modernity is enjoyed by Orlando as male; Victorian constraint is palpably a matter of surfaces, of appearances that are belied by the fact that despite time and gender change, she/he is one. That truth is phrased in every possible way in the course of the novel. Orlando really is male; really is female; is neither male nor female; is both male and female. Sapphic representation is closest to the surface of the text when Orlando, now a woman, disguises as a man to pick up a woman, Nell, to whom he reveals the truth. Countering what men say about women, that they care only for men, "Orlando professed great enjoyment in the society of her own sex, and leave it to the gentlemen to prove, as they are very fond of doing, that this is impossible" (161). "From the probity of breeches she turned to the seductiveness of petticoats and enjoyed the love of both sexes equally" (161). "Through all these changes she had remained, she reflected, fundamentally the same" (173). That fundamental sameness is the sameness of difference. And so, "She wrote. She wrote. She wrote" (196).

The materiality of the letter is this truth, the ardent yet tongue-in-cheek expression of *Orlando*. In a letter of December 26, 1924 to Jacques Raverat, to whom she often turned to think about sexuality, Woolf offers an account of Vita Sackville-West that boomerangs along the axes of identification and amusement that her novel traces too to its material sources, woods and words:

> [H]er real claim to consideration, is, if I may be so coarse, her legs. Oh they are exquisite — running like splendid pillars up into her trunk, which is that of a breastless cuirassier (yet she has 2 children) but all about her is virginal, savage, patrician; and why she writes, which she does with complete competency, and a pen of brass, is a puzzle to me. If I were she, I should merely stride, with Elk hounds, behind me, through my ancestral woods. She descends from Dorset, Buckingham, Sir Philip Sidney, and the whole of English history, which she keeps, stretched in coffins, one after another, from 1300 to the present day, under her dining room floor. (no. 1520; 3:149-50)

Woolf's claims to find the Elizabethan age in Knole, in Vita, the aristocratic embodiment of England and English literature, could be taken as some celebration of "heritage." Nonetheless, these are routes to what Woolf termed "moments of being" in her late autobiographical "A Sketch of the Past," when connections are made to some fundamental relation between things that nonetheless remain distinct: "[S]ome real thing behind appearances; and I make it real by putting it into words. It is only by putting it into words that I make it whole;...we — I mean all human beings — are connected with this;...we are the words;...we are the thing itself."[6]

Orlando finally does not have her great house; Woolf holds no brief for the Sackvilles — there is nothing remarkable about their background except insofar as attachment to it tropes a deeper attachment. From the opening page, when Orlando is seen "slicing the head of a Moor" (11), British imperialism is not ignored; courtly society is mocked. Vita Sackville-West's "The Land" is quoted in *Orlando*:

> And then I came to a field where the springing grass,
> Was dulled by the hanging cups of fritillaries,
> Sullen and foreign-looking, the snaky flower,
> Scarfed in dull purple, like Egyptian girls — (195)

6 Virginia Woolf, *Moments of Being*, edited by Jeanne Schulkind (New York: Harcourt, 1985), 72.

and immediately subject to scrutiny: "but—girls? Are girls necessary?" (195–6). Woolf draws attention to the incongruity of the orientalizing sapphism found in comparing flowers to "Egyptian girls." She dares, invites, the reader to see something that could have remained hidden under the guise of a seemingly innocuous exoticism (elsewhere mocked in Orlando's attachment to gypsies) that masks and encodes same-sex desire. The eroticized landscape in the poem is matched in *Orlando* in those moments when Orlando retreats from society to write, moments when the desire to merge with the landscape produces imaginative life and, at the same time, the desire to cease to be achieved by such a fusion (it is also in such a moment that the perfect marital partner appears). At the end of the novel, Orlando is ready to bury her poem, "The Oak Tree," at the base of the oak tree; instead, she leaves it lying there unburied, nominally doubling it, yet remaining separate from it.

* * *

At work on *Orlando,* Woolf reports herself "woolgathering away about Women and Fiction" (February 18, 1928; 3:175) for a talk she expects to give at Newnham College, Cambridge, a few months hence. It actually was delivered there on October 20, followed by another lecture a week later at Girton (Vita Sackville-West accompanied her on the latter occasion). By then, *Orlando* had been published; contrary to Woolf's expectations, it outsold *To the Lighthouse,* over 6000 copies by the end of December, as she notes in her diary (3:212); favorable reviews included one by Desmond MacCarthy in the *Sunday Times* on October 14; another by Hugh Walpole proclaimed it a masterpiece.[7] *A Room of One's Own* (1929) developed from "Women and Fiction" (a version of it was published under that title in the US). When it was finished a year later, Woolf characteristically anticipated the worst: "I shall be attacked for a feminist & hinted at for a sapphist" (October 23, 1929; 3:262). Once again

7 Early reviews are gathered in Robin Majumdar and Allen McLaurin, eds., *Virginia Woolf: The Critical Heritage* (London: Routledge & Kegan Paul, 1975).

she was proved wrong; by February it had sold 10,000 copies. Ethel Smyth wrote in its praise; she and Woolf had begun their "amorous unnatural friendship" (August 25, 1930), unnatural because while Ethel loved her, she did not love Ethel. Her diary captures Smyth's speech; Woolf's "I" becomes Smyth's: "I am to some extent Ethel's literary executor, a post I have always vaguely desired; & so I now make a few notes as she talks, for a portrait.... She said that she was a very brave woman. It is a quality I adore. And I have it. One of the bravest things I ever did was to tell people my age.... She was on her way — is now I suppose in the train or on the ship, this cold grey day — to Belfast, to conduct her Sea Songs (one of my best things)...(October 23, 1930; 3:325–6). Sapphism writes these identifications.

* * *

Woolf was pleased with the form of *A Room of One's Own*, "half talk half soliloquy"; it allowed her "to get more on to the page than any how else"; "made itself up" in bed, "& forced itself" on her (3:221). It recovers the terrain of *Orlando*, now as an argument combined in the compaction Woolf notes, an amalgam that requires fiction. Getting so much on the page coincides with doing more than one thing at once. Its condensation is signaled by opening in mid-sentence, mid-scene, mid-thought, and with a "But..." that continues and contradicts, "But, you may say," ventriloquizing the imagined objection of the other.[8] Invited to speak on women and fiction, she offers instead, as an equivalent, a room of one's own. How to get from one to the other? Only by recognizing that the topic prescribed has a number of possible meanings: a survey of English women's writing (quickly done, from Fanny Burney to Elizabeth Gaskell with Austen, the Brontës, George Eliot front and center and "some witticisms if possible about Miss Mitford" [3]). But it also might entail saying what women are like, or what fictions are told about them, or how they appear in fiction. Because no conclusion about these

---

8   Virginia Woolf, *A Room of One's Own*, edited by Susan Gubar (New York: Harcourt, 2005), 3. All subsequent citations are from this edition.

topics ever could be reached, Woolf prefers the concrete point, "a woman must have money and a room of her own if she is to write fiction" (4). This "nugget of pure truth" is deceptively single, and the route is fiction, for "fiction...is likely to contain more truth than fact" (4). As in *Orlando*, Woolf questions the regime of fact that is tied to the biographical, biological subject. Explicitly here "'I' is only a convenient term for somebody who has no real being" (4); the pseudonyms ventured to articulate her / their reflections are like fish out of water, itself a site of reflections, a surface that can be still as a glass or rippled and intractable. Fictions could be truer than fact because their coherence exceeds the ordinary demarcations separating one thing from another, or because, by effacing these demarcations they require an entire change of perception, one in which an "I" cannot be distinguished from the surface of reflection. The you Woolf addresses, answers, and ventriloquizes is not just you; it also is I, it is her.

These generalizations are pertinent to the shape of *A Room of One's Own*. It starts by seeming to argue for the intractable difference that gender difference makes (in making this argument Woolf seems fully to earn the feared label "feminist"), but closes with what is said ought to have been the opening sentence: "it is fatal for any one who writes to think of their sex. It is fatal to be a man or woman pure and simple; one must be woman-manly or man-womanly" (102–3). Apparently the question of woman and writing is solved by being dissolved. Yet the conjunctions (of man and woman) preserve the categories dissolved in combinations that nonetheless produces ones whose mirrored aspect is a chiasmic join. Another name for it might be the other feared label "Sapphist." Even as the first chapter ends, having detailed the impoverished educational status of women compared to men and all the exclusions enforced, the question of the relation of men and women takes the form of a pair of opposing observations: "I thought how unpleasant it is to be locked out; and I thought how it is worse perhaps to be locked in" (24). Male advantage, male imprisonment.

The boundary between male and female, Woolf ventures, is a trick mirror: men demean women as a way to assure themselves of their power, a Freudian possibility that Woolf takes in a

Lacanian direction to deconstruct the imaginary Phallus at the heart of the Symbolic. Remove this impediment and the boundary could disappear; the "freedom to think of things in themselves" (39) might arise. This possibility is not just a thought experiment; that's why women must have economic independence (figured as 500 pounds per annum) and a room where they may no longer be subjected to harassment; no longer be in relation to men, neither demeaned nor exalted, either way belied when valued as mothers and wives trapped in Kantian marriages made for the benefit of men. Nonetheless, the freedom Woolf advocates remains a relation; for free, women are in a different way in the position of being everything and nothing: the difference lies in the advantage of non-being (of being outside of, or beside, the differential of all or nothing, all and nothing, created by absolutizing male–female difference). Non-being, non-possessiveness, and anonymity is the way of being in relation to "things in themselves." A room of one's own is a paradoxical place; it could be where one is locked up, as Woolf imagines was the condition of early modern English women writers, scribbling for their own amusement under the benign disposition of indulgent, financially-secure aristocratic husbands, and freed from the burden of maternity.

Most women are poor; to rail against constraint, to write in anger is self-defeating in just the opposite direction from the self-liberation Woolf advocates as the freedom of a self-discovery and self-expression possible when there is no "I" — "I" created by conditions of harassment, hatred, self-aggrandizement, and demeaning. "When people compare Shakespeare and Jane Austen" (Woolf is one of the people who has just done that), "they may mean that the minds of both had consumed all impediments; and for that reason we do not know Jane Austen and we do not know Shakespeare, and for that reason Jane Austen pervades every word that she wrote, and so does Shakespeare" (67).

Shakespeare is over and again Woolf's name for the state of mind Woolf desires; she conjures his equally talented sister who never wrote a word and died in abject circumstances as his opposite. The story does not end there: "All women together ought to let flowers fall upon the tomb of Aphra Behn" (65),

she wrote "on equal terms with men" (63). So doing, Behn did not become a man but a different kind of woman, a different kind of mother — one who models, generates women who write themselves into the existence "Things in themselves" inhabit, "the presence of reality" (109), a presence that is the present possibility in which Shakespeare's sister still lives, "for great poets do not die" (112).

This present lies within and ahead, 100 years hence, Woolf imagines. It is not yet time for Sappho again (citing Swinburne, Sappho almost appears in the text [65]), but for the novel, the form that emerged in the eighteenth and nineteenth centuries as if for women; in seeming to offer a mirror of life (of heterosexuality as historical truth), it also, formally, offered something in conflict with this so-called realism, "something that is not life...something that one calls integrity...truth" (71). This univocity exceeds or sidesteps the conflict that dualism and division suggest. Woolf sums it up in the readerly experience that takes the form of saying to oneself, "But this is what I have always felt and known and desired!" (71).

What is this? Who is this "I"? There is no simple answer to that question. On the one hand, it certainly belongs to a woman who has thought her way past patriarchal constrictions and has the means to do so. That woman is a woman but "a woman who has forgotten that she is a woman" (91), if that word means the person constructed through invidious differences between men and women. The way of being "a woman who has forgotten that she is a woman" that Woolf enjoins is the way to be a woman writer: "[S]he wrote as a woman, but as a woman who has forgotten that she is a woman." Writing, however literally meant, tropes a way of being in the world. This nonetheless is a way of being a woman: Woolf contends always that men and women are not the same and that "it would be a thousand pities if women wrote like men, or lived like men, or looked like men" (86). On the other hand (how many hands now?), Woolf proposes that what women must do now is the unprecedented task of writing for and from the relations of women to women summed up in the minimal, explosive sentence, "Chloe liked Olivia..." (80), where the ellipsis leaves unsaid what is to be said and thereby begins to say it when this conjunction of liking and likening becomes the occasion for Woolf to introduce and disavow at the same time the name of Sir Chartres Biron, the magistrate overseeing the obscenity trial launched against Radclyffe Hall's *Well of Loneliness*. (Woolf testified on its behalf; the trial is a significant context for the writing of *Orlando* and *A Room of One's Own*.)

Thinking woman by way of sapphism is not the endpoint of Woolf's inquiry into the relationships between sex and gender and sexuality; she arrives at androgyny (that first sentence that comes late in the text), the fusion that effaces and preserves difference, Woolf's bottom-line reality principle that brings Woolf's feminist and sapphist project to an end in which she deplores sex-consciousness that makes for division; it is those categories that the book both affirms and takes apart in the name of the reality called fiction. Only male writers in the line of Shakespeare, Woolf affirms, have thus far inhabited the androgyny she values. "In our time Proust was wholly androgynous, if not perhaps a little too much a woman. But that failing is too rare for one to complain of it" (102), though it may explain the war against buggers to which Woolf alludes often in her diary, her "anti-bugger revolution," as she termed it in an entry on April 19, 1925 (3:10).

* * *

November 27, 1925. Woolf imagines that her "life would cease" (3:48) if her six most beloved intimates were to die: her husband, her sister (Nessa is necessity), Vanessa's husband Clive Bell, her lover Duncan Grant (himself often the lover of men), Lytton Strachey, and Morgan (Forster).

* * *

August 31, 1928. "Morgan was here for the week end; timid, touchy, infinitely charming. One night we got drunk, & talked of sodomy, & sapphism…. This was started by Radclyffe Hall & her meritorious dull book…. Morgan said that Dr Head can convert the sodomites. 'Would you like to be converted?' Leonard asked. 'No' said Morgan, quite definitely. He said he thought

Sapphism disgusting; partly from convention, partly because he disliked that women should be independent of men" (3:193).

* * *

November 5?, 1930. "Hugh Walpole to tea...his piteous, writhing & wincing & ridiculous & flaying alive story of Willie Maugham's portrait.... Thats what I cant get over. For instance I cant tell you all the meanings there are to me in his saying I was like a man in love with a duchess — (the meaning is that Hugh is in love with a male opera singer). Would you mind Virginia? (this said past midnight, Vita & I alone) And I said I should" (3:328).

The Bechdel Test

The Bechdel test gets its name from a 1985 comic, *The Rule*, an early installment in Alison Bechdel's long-running series, *Dykes to Watch Out For*. The initial frame pictures a movie marquee showing *The Rule* (and offering thanks to Liz Wallace, whom Bechdel credits with the idea). Two women, unnamed, are seen walking past theaters with other offerings on their marquees — all apparently action movies: *The Mercenary, The Barbarian, The Vigilante,* and, finally, *Rambo Meets Godzilla*. The blond proposes they go to see one; the woman with short-cropped dark hair responds with her rule about which films she will see: "It has to have at least two women in it...who...**talk** to each other about...something besides a **man**," a daunting prospect given what seems available. The strip has an unexpected punchline or two in response to the dilemma. The last film she was able to see, she continues, was *Alien*. It satisfied the rule; the two women in it (Ripley and Lambert) talk about the monster; describing them, the animated speaker fills the frame with a gesture meant perhaps to conjure up the monster. The two women continue their walk side by side in a frame that matches an earlier one, but now they seem stymied by the chance of finding a film to see. The blond ventures instead that they go to her place; her offer is accepted enthusiastically. Sex seems likely to be in view. *Alien* and the monster between the two women perhaps translates what they are about to do. That the two appear to be a cross-race couple adds to the tongue-in-cheek frisson.

By itself, *Alien* (1979; directed by Ridley Scott) is a witty solution to the dilemma the two women face; although it is an action film, with a predominantly male crew, it is only Ripley (believe it or not; her name perhaps nods in the direction of Patricia Highsmith) who escapes. She is the "final girl" figure Carol Clover identifies in *Men, Women, and Chainsaws*,[1] with the further twist that the "monster" is not a predatory male that the "final girl" survives to defeat. Does it have a gender? The thing it seems intent on doing is not so much the destruction of the crew as its own reproduction; it seems to have a number of ways of doing that — fields of pods, egglike plants (when touched, a creature bursts from one to suck face, impregnating Kane, one of the male crew members, who dies giving birth to another creature); other victims are bound in cocoons, gestating. It is probably premature to wonder whether the Ripley of *Alien* is a dyke to watch out for, although she does almost miss her chance to escape because she can't find her cat, Jones; too soon too to wonder if in sequels she will want to ask the monster, "Are You My Mother?" The hint is given, however, in the film; the computer in charge of the mission is called "Mother." "Mother" is intent on saving the life the monster mother creates, and is quite indifferent to human life.

No explicit connection to *Alien* can be found in Bechdel's 2012 graphic novel *Are You My Mother?*, although its subtitle, *A Comic Drama*, gestures at the generic mashup it shares with the film. The film passes the Bechdel test; whether it is legible as feminist/sapphic, as *The Rule* certainly is, remains a question. Literary allusion is one route from the early strip to the novel, as was also the case in Bechdel's first graphic novel *Fun Home: A Family Tragicomic* (2006).[2] The Wikipedia entry for "Bechdel test" credits Virginia Woolf's *A Room of One's Own* as Bechdel's inspiration for the rule, citing a passage from chapter 5, just after the project for the modern novel is announced in the stark, pregnant predication, "Chloe liked Olivia": "All these relationships between women, I thought, rapidly recalling the

---

1   Carol J. Clover, *Men, Women, and Chainsaws: Gender in the Modern Horror Film* (Princeton, NJ: Princeton University Press, 1997).
2   On this, see the review of *Fun Home: A Family Tragicomic* by Michael Moon in the September 2006 issue of *Guttergeek: The Discontinuous Review of Graphic Narrative,* http://guttergeek.com/archives/2006/page78/funhome/funhome.html.

splendid gallery of fictitious women, are too simple...and I tried to remember any case in the course of my reading where two women are represented as friends.... They are now and then mothers and daughters. But almost without exception they are shown in their relation to men. It was strange to think that all the great women of fiction were, until Jane Austen's day, not only seen by the other sex, but seen only in relation to the other sex. And how small a part of a woman's life is that..." (*A Room of One's Own*, 81).

Woolf's excitement at what the imaginary novel she is describing might achieve is palpable; it is not just its subject matter of women in relation to each other, "a sight that has never been seen since the world began" (83), but that its realization would create an as-yet-unrealized world; it "would be to talk of something else, looking steadily out of the window...in the shortest of shorthand, in words that are hardly syllabled yet...to devise some entirely new combination of her resources...to absorb the new into the old without disturbing the infinitely intricate and elaborate balance of the whole" (82). This may be the ambition of Bechdel's practice in its combination of word and image. In her introduction to *The Essential Dykes to Watch Out For*,[3] Bechdel modestly, self-deprecatingly credits her achievement to her inability to succeed as an artist (she was rejected from art school) and her limited success as a writer; she cherishes a rejection letter from Adrienne Rich for an autobiographical piece she submitted to *Sinister Wisdom*, while a fan letter, years later, from Rich about her cartoon series affirms how well she succeeded by combining her resources. *Are You My Mother?* realizes the world in which its words take place: recurring scenes of Alison on the phone with her mother or in therapy with Jocelyn or Carol are filled in with the details of time and place thanks to Bechdel's exacting drawing. Nothing is simply one thing, to recall the sentence from *To the Lighthouse* (1927; "For nothing was simply one thing") that serves as the epigraph to Bechdel's deeply recursive book.[4]

3 Alison Bechdel, *The Essential Dykes to Watch Out For* (New York: Houghton Mifflin Harcourt, 2008).
4 Parenthetical citations are from Alison Bechdel, *Are You My Moth-*

Allusions to Woolf are dense in Bechdel's text. Crucially, she recalls a moment in Woolf's late "A Sketch of the Past" (printed in *Moments of Being*). We see Bechdel reading that volume, pen in her mouth, as she thinks about how much more she imagines herself in her mother's mind than she probably is (18). How to effect their separation — how to get out of a feedback loop that often becomes one with no way out: Woolf's way, she reports, and Bechdel quotes, lay in writing *To the Lighthouse*: "[O]ne day walking round Tavistock Square I made up, as I sometimes make up my books, *To the Lighthouse*; in a great, apparently involuntary rush...when it was written I ceased to be obsessed by my mother" (*Moments of Being,* 81). Nothing is simply one thing on this page with its juxtaposition of Bechdel and her mother, Woolf and Julia Stephen. In the frame that completes the page, showing Alison with her therapist Carol, the pen that was in Bechdel's mouth at the top right of the page is in Carol's hand at the bottom left; Woolf's profile on the cover of the first edition of *Moments of Being* is answered by Alison's below; Alison is not talking to her therapist about her mother, although the banner above the frame indicates that she has been in therapy her entire adult life because she has yet to lay her "deeply felt emotion" about her "to rest"; inside the frame, she remarks on her solid but precarious relation with her lover and on the book she is engaged in, writing about her father's suicide. As she reports towards the end of *Are You My Mother?*, it was while in the midst of "intense creative ferment" (253), working simultaneously on her comic strip (in which "one of my characters has just gotten pregnant") and on *Fun Home,* while reading intensively in psychoanalytic theory (the cover of an Adam Phillips title appears at this point), that she felt "the very first stirrings of this book about my mother." The scene of "conception" is this flood of coincidences.

Metaphorically, these multiple things — writing/drawing; comics; novels; Woolf; psychoanalysis, on the page, on the couch — are condensed in the figuration of maternal conception.

er?: A Comic Drama (New York: Houghton Mifflin Harcourt, 2012); see Virginia Woolf, *To the Lighthouse* (New York: Harcourt, 1981), 186, for Bechdel's epigraph.

On the opening page of *Are You My Mother?*, in an image worthy of *Alien,* Bechdel explains how she "understood reproduction as a child. I was an egg inside my mother and she was still an egg inside her mother, and so forth and so on" (7). The task of creating involves breaking out of this "dizzying infinite regress" without beginning or end. "There's a certain relief in knowing that I am a terminus," Bechdel reports (7). But a terminus, an end point, also is a place where one can make new connections, get off one train and board another. The metaphor of maternal reproduction shuts down the process belied in the very fact of the writing/drawing, producing an object that is neither Alison Bechdel nor her mother; the moment in the narrative when they communicate best is when they speak lines written by someone else, Oscar Wilde, in fact (241). Bechdel concludes that "by stepping back a bit from the real thing to look at it, that we are most present" (242).

It's a conclusion worthy of Woolf. In *To the Lighthouse,* Mrs. Ramsay makes the present by bringing people together for the possibility of an experience that is not simply theirs, not just a matter of individual consciousness or of conscious desire. Woolf makes clear that this way of living is an aesthetic project by assigning it to the figure of Lily Briscoe, trying to capture in her painting what Woolf attempts in words. Lily is not part of the Ramsay family; she too is a terminus, an unmarried woman; she conveys the life of the Ramsays in geometrical forms on canvas. *Are You My Mother?* draws on a number of psychoanalytical texts, Lacan's mirror stage among them, but mainly on essays by D.W. Winnicott (and Bechdel's research into his life). Winnicott read Woolf; the connection Bechdel traces is by way of James Strachey, translator of Freud, Winnicott's analyst, and the youngest brother of Woolf's beloved Lytton. They cross paths, unknowingly, on two pages of Bechdel's book (24–5) — Woolf strolls, making it up, in Tavistock Square as the young Winnicott rushes by on the way to Strachey's couch.

* * *

In a diary entry that Bechdel cites (November 28, 1928), Woolf records that had her father lived longer, "his life would have entirely ended mine" (3:208); a year later (December 14, 1929), she notes that had she married Strachey, she would "never have written anything" (3:273). Late in *Are You My Mother?*, Bechdel recounts that while researching Winnicott she had yet to tell her mother that her "book about him" also was to be about her (197). Is Winnicott Bechdel's mother? Bechdel acknowledges that is her desire (21); it is based perhaps on identification—Bechdel credits Alice Miller's claim that therapists often were children who responded to their mother's neediness by mothering them, as Bechdel thinks she herself has done. "I want Jocelyn to be my mother," she writes as well (51). Jocelyn breaks a (therapeutic) rule when she tells Bechdel that she lost her mother when young (as Woolf did) and that it took years for her to get over it. She breaks another, and would do it again, she tells Bechdel years after therapy ended, when she tells Alison that she is adorable (273–4), a sentence she wanted her mother to say. *Are You My Mother?* asks its reader to occupy that place. Am I your mother?

* * *

In the "Cartoonist's Introduction" to *The Essential Dykes to Watch Out For*, Bechdel reports that until she began that project she only drew men (xiii). At the end of the introduction, contemplating her accomplishment in the decades-long series, she wonders whether in answering the call of Adrienne Rich to "speak the unspeakable" (xviii; an admonition that echoes Woolf's call to find "words that are hardly syllabled yet"), she had made lesbians conventional. "Have I churned out episodes of this comic strip every two weeks for **decades** to prove that we're the same as everyone else?" Does (God forbid) *The Essential Dykes to Watch Out For* essentialize dykes? There is, I would venture to say, more than one way to essentialize. If Bechdel's book succeeds in the mold that Woolf provides, it does so by showing that nothing is one thing, and/but that nonetheless there is, as Woolf puts it in *To the Lighthouse*, something "between things, beyond things" that lends them "some common feeling" (192). There is, in short, a life in common that allows each thing to be itself and yet not itself, same and different, at once.

12

"The Wise Sappho"

In her prose tribute, "The Wise Sappho," H.D. locates Sappho's wisdom in the double-seeing rooted in the sweet bitterness of erotic experience. The form it takes for H.D. is expressed most directly in Fragment 57, translated first by H.D. in her prose piece: "What country girl bewitches your heart who knows not how to draw her skirt about her ankles?"[1] The poem can be taken to be self-addressed, mocking herself for a desire so much beneath her, yet finding that this simple country girl bewitches her. Anne Carson translates "bewitches" with the phrase "seduces your wits": some kind of thinking otherwise is involved. H.D. elaborates: "It is for the strange almost petulant little phrases that we value this woman" (60). In Fragment 160, Sappho claims (H.D. translates), "I sing and I sing beautifully like this, in order to please my friends — my girl-friends" (62). The poems bewitch us, inviting us, through the particularity of their severe observations, to see something else. "She constructed from the simple gestures of a half-grown awkward girl, a being, a companion, an equal" (65).

Hard specificity attaches to each of the many "girl-friends" in the fragments. H.D. summons their names; details suggest an entirety to her; for Atthis, for instance, a typology emerges, a biography of the beloved, adored, but perhaps not worth

---

1 H.D., *Notes on Thought and Vision & The Wise Sappho* (San Francisco, CA: City Lights, 1982), 59. All subsequent citations of H.D. are to this volume. Her *Collected Poems 1912–1944*, edited by Louis Martz (New York: New Directions, 1983), contains poems inspired by Fragments 36, 40, 41, 68, and 113.

adoration, a betrayer, unfaithful. "You have gone to Andromeda" (Fragment 131): she embodies the force of Eros the bittersweet: "I loved you, Atthis, once long ago / a little child you seemed to me and graceless" (Fragment 49). Sappho provides the small, petty detail in her sculpted lines: "She constructed perfect and flawless (as in her verse, she carved from current Aeolian dialect, immortal phrases) the whole, the perfection, the undying spirit of goddess, muse or sacred being from the simple grace of some tall half-developed girl" (65). Sappho, imagiste avant la lettre.

For H.D., Sappho accomplishes something akin to what the art critic Adrian Stokes found essential to artistic creation as he parsed it in *Michelangelo: A Study in the Nature of Art*, "a firm alliance between generality and the obdurate otherness of objects" that Stokes rephrases as "the suggestion of oneness, and the insistence on the reality of otherness if only by the self-inclusive object-character of the artefact itself."[2] Sappho the wise sees in these cruel, ungainly girls wisdom, perfection — identification. Stokes takes as an example a late drawing of Michelangelo's (no. 441), perhaps his last, as Frederick Hartt speculates in his entry in his catalogue, describing the drawing this way: "[T]he essential forms of Mother and Child unite in a blinding embrace," and completing his thought with lines of verse, "Extinguish sight and speech, / Each on each."[3] Stokes writes: "Just as the child is embedded in the mother, so she herself is embedded, it appears, in a homogeneous material which discloses her form, as might the adumbration of drapery" (72). The lines that suggest they are two also join them as one, making them manifestations of the line, "a homogeneous material," Stokes intimates, like a single folded fabric.

---

2 Adrian Stokes, *Michelangelo: A Study in the Nature of Art* (London: Tavistock Publications, 1955), 66–7. Stokes was earlier a close friend of Ezra Pound's; H.D. had been Pound's fiancée; Stokes was analyzed by Melanie Klein, H.D. by Freud.

3 Frederick Hartt, *Michelangelo Drawings* (New York: Abrams, 1970), 309.

In Sappho, oneness takes form in the distributed name "Cleis"; she is, it seems, Sappho's mother in Fragment 98, her daughter in Fragment 132. Fragment 98 comes in two pieces: the first recalls how her mother said that when she was young, her beauty — or any girl's beauty — was enhanced by having her hair bound in purple. 98B addresses Cleis; Sappho tells her she has no such spangled hair band to give her. Is the Cleis she addresses her mother or a girl she wishes she could similarly adorn to make her thereby an avatar of her mother? Sappho's daughter is explicitly named Cleis; Fragment 132 breaks off in the middle of an unfinished comparison of this daughter to someone else "in exchange for whom I would not" — would not what? Cleis is said to be "like golden flowers"; in 98 the purple band is refigured as "spangled" — golden? How does one thing become another and yet remain itself? "Cleis" asks that question by way of a name that may be called maternal.

H.D. opens "The Wise Sappho" by recalling a line from the *Palatine Anthology* that sums up Sappho's poetic accomplishment in the phrase "little, but all roses" (57). Not so, says H.D., unless by roses the color is meant, a red that conveys the passion of the poet's lines. Or is their color rather gold, she wonders; or is it both, or neither? After all, "it is not warmth we look for," but something else that conveys the heat of passion at the same time as it negates it, as well as whatever qualities or color roses might convey. It is not this, nor that, yet this, yet that, but this, but that: in these conjunctions, H.D. phrases the relationships of two things at once. The double grammar she finds in Sappho — or in the name "Cleis" — is a "white, inhuman element" (57). "Sappho has become for us a name, an abstraction as well as a pseudonym for poignant human feeling," H.D. concludes (67). This summary statement of opposing identifications prompts her to recall that Plato venerated Sappho as wise.

In closing, H.D. finally endorses Meleager's phrase "little, but all roses" as true — it means that "Sappho" names at once inhuman abstraction and is a pseudonym for human feeling; her sentence continues: "[S]he is indeed rocks set in a blue sea, she is the sea itself, breaking and tortured and torturing, but never broken. She is the island of artistic perfection" (67). H.D. had made this final move from roses to rocks at the opening of her tribute. There, she describes the fragments as rocks "between which flowers by some chance may grow but which endure when the staunch blossoms have perished" (58); the roses grow from the enduring rocks. The poem as object, like human relations as object relations, exists beyond the human. Stokes says that the art object is "a Whole, that nevertheless refers beyond itself without breaking the entirety" (19). Ultimately, this claim leads Stokes to the stones (inhuman white marble) that Michelangelo opens in his sculpture and conceptualized in his poetry: sonnet 151 declares that the artist has no idea in mind — no conception ("alcun concetto") — that the stone does not circumscribe within itself.[4] H.D. might not have thought of Michelangelo when she described the artwork as living stone, but she does mention Leonardo's *Madonna of the Rocks* in "Notes on Thought and Vision" as exemplifying how the artistic idea becomes a physical thing. "The *Madonna of the Rocks* is not a picture. It is a window," H.D. writes (18); not a window on the world but one that manifests the conjunction of mind and body, a conception.

* * *

The *Madonna of the Rocks* is the name of two paintings by Leonardo, one in the National Gallery in London (see Fig. 3), the other in the Louvre. Art historians worry their dating and their authenticity. I am concerned with other doublings found in both of them. To the Madonna and Child, Leonardo has added the not entirely unexpected figure of the infant John the Baptist paying homage to the newborn Jesus. Balancing him there is a winged figure usually identified as an angel; in the Paris version his finger points at the baby Baptist; the hand gesture is missing in the London version, where his drapery is more subdued as well. The angel is a somewhat anomalous figure; I refer to him as "him," but his face has that "androgynous" quality often ascribed to Leonardo's figures (Marcel Duchamp added a mustache to the Mona Lisa). One doubling in the painting involves

---

4 See Michelangelo, *The Poems*, edited and translated by Christopher Ryan (London: J.M. Dent, 1996), 138–9, for the text and translation.

Figure 3. Leonardo da Vinci, *The Virgin of the Rocks* (about 1491/2–9 and 1506–8), National Gallery, London.

the question of whether gender is distributed as two separate kinds or as one. An answer perhaps lies in the other doubling so conspicuous that it has come to name the paintings, the rocks.

To say they form a background hardly begins to describe them. The human and divine figures are set within the rocks. Skin tones relate to their browns illuminated by the light that falls on both. Foliage between the rocks and bodies is in a grisaille akin to the wisps of the Madonna's hair; rocks fold like drapery. Apertures in the rocks lead to a distant prospect where they fade to gray; folds and depths are matched by the extraordinary golden drapery that swathes the Virgin's midsection, opening a pocket that suggests depths similarly unfathomable. Perhaps this conspicuously highlighted center of the painting suggests its origin; it is akin to the drapery Stokes summoned up for a simile to describe the embeddedness of figures in form that suggests at once their separation and their fusion. In the *Madonna of the Rocks*, what ensures it not being a picture, as H.D. averred, and thereby discloses the "inhuman element" that she affirms, are the rocks through which a vision of life is nonetheless disclosed.

Kenneth Clark closes a discussion of the enigmas in another painting of Leonardo's, the *Madonna and Child with St. Anne* in the Louvre, by summoning up the *Madonna of the Rocks*, contextualizing it by way of a passage he quotes from one of Leonardo's notebooks: "The earth has a spirit of growth. Its flesh is the soil, its bones the stratifications of the rocks which forms the mountains, its blood the springs of water; and the increase and decrease of blood in the pulses is represented in the earth by the ebb and flow of the sea."[5] "Everything comes from everything, and everything is made from everything," Leonardo depends upon Anaxagoras to affirm (14); microcosm and macrocosm are both entirely elemental. "Spirit" exists only in bodies: "The

---

5 Kenneth Clark, *Looking at Pictures* (New York: Holt, Rinehart and Winston, 1960), 164. Clark does not footnote this citation from Leic. 34r; a fuller translation can be found in *The Notebooks of Leonardo da Vinci*, edited by Edward McCurdy (New York: George Braziller, 1958), 86. The next sentence reads: "And the vital heat of the world is fire which is spread throughout the earth." This passage is not found in the *Selections from the Notebooks of Leonardo da Vinci*, edited by Irma A. Richter (London: Oxford University Press, 1952), from which I quote below.

Figure 4. Leonardo da Vinci, *The Burlington House Cartoon* (about 1499-1500), National Gallery, London.

soul's desire is to remain with its body, because without the organic instruments of that body it can neither act nor feel" (281). Bodies, as Leonardo's *sfumato* shows, are not ultimately separated from each other; edges touch. "The limitation of one body is that which begins another" (125). From Leonardo's writing, Clark draws this conclusion:

> Everything in nature, even the solid-seeming earth, was in a state of flux. But the source and centre of this continuous energy remained mysterious to him. He could only symbolise it by this ideal construction, in which forms, themselves suggestive of further lives, flow in and out of one another with inexhaustible energy; and at the apex of this vital pyramid is the head of Leonardo's angel-familiar, smiling, half with love for human creatures and half with the knowledge of a vital secret which they can never possess. (164)

The "vital secret" of the angel — the secret of the vitality of the artwork — is perhaps available in the cartoon that shares the room in the Salisbury Wing of the National Gallery where the *Madonna of the Rocks* currently is hung (see Fig. 4). The Burlington Cartoon shows, once again, the Madonna and Child and the infant John. But in this depiction, the Virgin sits on her mother's lap. St Anne looks at Mary. Mother is not visibly older than her daughter; they are versions of each other, like the Cleis Sappho multiplied. Behind the figures rocky mountains are suggested; St. Anne's finger points upward, as if it were a peak in front of the background terrain; it points our thoughts. This cartoon is related to the Louvre *Madonna and Child with St. Anne*; there, a lamb substitutes for the Baptist. Jesus embraces it, his mother embraces him. She sits on her mother's lap; Anne looks down on the scene. Her head is one with the mountains in the background, the top of her head the highest peak in the triangle formed by the figures, themselves composed of triangular shapes, draped bodies that match the shapes of mountains. Freud famously saw his infamously mistranslated vulture mother as the key to the psycho-sexuality of the artist displayed in this painting. His error nonetheless points to a truth of fusion of forms and bodies, if not of his reductive formula of the "blending of male and female natures" by which Freud designated the essence of male homosexuality by way of maternal identification, while almost conceding that such unions are found in everyone.[6]

6   See Sigmund Freud, *Leonardo da Vinci and a Memory of His Child-*

Mother and daughter are fused in Leonardo's cartoon and painting. Mother and son are fused in that late Michelangelo drawing mentioned above, while an early drawing (no. 57), inspired by Leonardo, shows the Virgin on her mother's lap. Michelangelo's last sculpture, the *Rondanini Pietà,* spectacularly, heartwrenchingly displays this fusion as the sculptor's attempt to find what lies in the rock he hews. An arm, polished, hangs detached, discarded from the bodies that yet emerge, barely formed, from the marble block. As Stokes says, "[T]he upright dead Christ is supposedly supported from behind by the Madonna...there is the effect, none the less, that the second figure rides on the back of the first" (85). As his language suggests, the erect dead figure is being taken from behind by the phantasmatic maternal form. Active aggression, passive reception, bisexuality, are terms for this union offered by Stokes. As one walks round this extraordinary sculpture in the Spanish Hospital in Milan's Sforza Castle, the relation of two-in-oneness, the separations, the fusions, and the emotional relations involved, keep changing — hugging, falling, standing, parting and joining all at once. Were this statue "finished" it would only be to be hacked away further. As Michelangelo puts it in poem 152, by removing, the sculptor places a living figure in the stone that grows precisely where the stone grows less, effaced, until having become nothing that one could name, it would achieve the perfection that Stokes calls "identity in difference" (17), "identity with the pulse of things" (15).

hood, translated by Alan Tyson (New York: W.W. Norton, 1964), 99. For an acute discussion, see Richard Halpern, *Shakespeare's Perfume: Sodomy and Sublimity in the Sonnets, Wilde, Freud, and Lacan* (Philadelphia: University of Pennsylvania Press, 2002), chap. 3.

13

Sister Outsider

In "Reclaiming Sodom," a piece that originally appeared in the short-lived zine *Queer Fuckers Monthly,* published under the auspices of Queer Nation Utah between 1990 and 1992, Rocky O'Donovan opens by expressing his envy of lesbians "because of one simple but vital factor of their existence; they have Lesbos — actual space which they can dream of and re-create and hope toward."[1] He proposes for "all of us Queer Boys" the project that names his essay: "I want to reclaim Sodom... — and really, it is ours whether we want it or not," a site of holocaust perpetrated by the "power-hungry, White, jealous, heterosexual, bourgeois, able-bodied, male god" whose actions are not confined to the biblical record. O'Donovan frames his call to reclaim Sodom in a number of ways, including a consideration of the possibility that the story in Genesis might not be condemning homosex but discrimination against strangers: this sin of inhospitality, he notes, is repeated when queers are condemned by the Mormon church that is one object of O'Donovan's polemic. In noting that the fire that destroyed Sodom was holocaustal, O'Donovan gestures to a link between discrimination against gays and anti-Semitism. Calling himself a "Sodomite-American," he affiliates with ethnic minorities that also use such hyphenated identities to claim a place in a nation

---

1   I cite from the reprinting of Rocky O'Donovan in Goldberg (ed.), *Reclaiming Sodom,* 247–8 (New York: Routledge, 1994). The piece came to title the anthology after Routledge balked on the title I had been commissioned to do, *The Sodomy Reader.*

that would exclude them and have done so, African-Americans most notably.

These alignments sit with and yet athwart O'Donovan's envy of lesbians. Where does Lot's wife figure? O'Donovan turns her into "a phallic pillar of salt, as a reminder of the power of the Almighty Penis." Lot's wife is joined thereby to gay men as the object of a male power both misogynistic and homophobic. Lesbians who "have" Lesbos appear to be unrelated to Lot's wife, as if they existed on some other planet than Queer Boys do, or were immune to the Judaeo-Christian legacy that leaves them — leaves us — with only Sodom as our home, Heimat.

O'Donovan issues a moving call to accept our excoriation and to make a home there; gestures of affiliation are simply that, its envy of the home lesbians can claim a piece of wit even if it does point to a place and time — in antiquity — when home was not a holocaust for faggots. Nonetheless, a comparison of the texts that remain under the names of Homer and Sappho puts a damper on O'Donovan's dream identification. All Lesbians are not lesbians, of course, and vice versa; lesbians don't necessarily imagine themselves in diaspora from Lesbos.

The connection O'Donovan envies is refused quite pointedly by Michelle Cliff in "Caliban's Daughter: The Tempest and the Teapot," a 1991 essay related to the project that titles her first book, *Claiming an Identity They Taught Me to Despise* (1980).[2] Cliff owns herself as black despite being taught to pass as white in her native Jamaica. The essay in which she names herself Caliban's daughter focuses on her sexuality, asking "what does it mean to love another woman — psychically and physically — in the Caribbean landscape?" Her answer: "One must first discard the word *lesbian*, then its location on an island off the coast of Turkey, in a Parisian restaurant, on an English country estate, in a postfeminist bar in Greenwich Village, in a music video" (48).

---

[2] I cite from Michelle Cliff, "Caliban's Daughter: The Tempest and the Teapot," *Frontiers: A Journal of Women Studies* 12, no. 2 (1991): 36–51, http://dx.doi.org/10.2307/3346845. For further discussion, see my *Tempest in the Caribbean* (Minneapolis: University of Minnesota Press, 2004), 70–9.

Cliff removes "lesbian" from her vocabulary as she searches for terms of self-identification. This entails disidentification with the miseducation of a colonial upbringing that insisted she think of herself as British and not know her past — slavery, Africa, the precolonial Caribbean. She seeks ways of writing "beyond a dissertation on intellectual game-playing in the Italian Renaissance" that she produced at the Warburg Institute "negotiated through six Western languages" (38). Her route requires the realization of her speechlessness about the identity she was taught not to know. Cliff opens paths in western texts to the voiceless and the unvoiced in them, leading her to identify with Victor, the wild boy; Bertha, the madwoman in the attic; Heathcliff, a former slave. Caribbean authors and artists like Aimé Césaire, Jean Rhys, Dionne Brand, and Ana Mendiata are invoked. Although she calls herself Caliban's daughter, this is a way to her grandmother Sycorax (Caliban has no named father), and through her to a masculinity not male as well as to a primordial attachment to place. "*Ruination*" names this, the Jamaican English for land that has been left uncultivated, allowed to return to its decolonized state; it houses the ruin of the nation and the island upon which the native can stand, "the granddaughter of Sycorax, precolonial female, landscape, I(s) land: I land" (40). This "I" is not singular — a self, a place — nor is it articulated in the language that would suppress it or that could name it only in denigration. "What does it mean when the Jamaican tomboy says, 'I am Heathcliff?' Or finds herself drawn to Bertha when she is told to identify with Jane?" (44).

One answer to the first question: it is to identify with Cathy and, at the same time, as the black male protagonist, therefore to refuse the western, colonial dichotomy of absolute dual gender differentiation. Cliff answers her second question when, thinking of Bertha, she recalls "the notion of the lesbian as monster, marauder; the man/woman in the closet" (48). Cliff's refusal of "lesbian" is not so much the denial of such associations (they are reclaimed) as it is a rejection of "lesbian" as "a heavy-handed emblem of western decadence, the seduction of the tropics by Europe, the colonization of the dark woman by the white one" (48). Refusing Lesbos as home or origin allows her sexuality to be something other than a western, colonial invention. Gesturing in the direction of a Caribbean island far more tolerant than others, Cliff momentarily entertains the possibility of substituting "Trinidadian" for "lesbian": "Trinidadians would not approve, especially if the suggestion came from a Jamaican" (48). Such renaming would be another appropriation; one locale cannot be substituted for another without ignoring the various histories of each place, of each inhabitant, singular only insofar as their identities are multiple. Cliff describes herself as "of Afro-Caribbean — Indian (Arawak and Carib), African, European — experience and heritage, and western experience and education" (40). These divisions are encapsulated in the name of the heroine of her first two novels, Clare Savage, "savage" in ancestry (misnaming the inheritance Cliff would trace to Sycorax or the historical Maroon leader Nanny), while her given, proper name looks no further than her skin for a bleaching that needs to be replaced by what has been effaced, the rapes of body and mind that produce the colonial subject.

Cliff's rejection of "lesbian" is anything but a repudiation of her sexuality. Without providing a name for it, she celebrates herself as a native of the islands "where to image oneself in another woman, to connect psychically and physically with another female, can be an act of empowerment, a step toward describing oneself in a new language (or, perhaps, an old language), being *self*ish (in my girlhood the thing I was never supposed to be)" (48).

* * *

Cliff's first book has an epigraph from the initial appearance of Audre Lorde's "Poetry Is Not a Luxury"; her next collection of prose and poetry, *The Land of Look Behind* (1985), is dedicated to Lorde, who, in turn, acknowledges Cliff in her "biomythography" *Zami: A New Spelling of My Name*.[3] Lorde's renaming derives from the vocabulary of Carriacou, the Caribbean island

---

3 Michelle Cliff, *The Land of Look Behind: Prose and Poetry* (Ithaca, NY: Firebrand Books, 1985). Audre Lorde, *Zami: A New Spelling of My Name* (Freedom, CA: Crossing Press, 1982).

where her mother was born. "*Zami. A Carriacou name for women who work together as friends and lovers,*" she defines it in the epilogue (255), "*Madivine. Friendling. Zami. How Carriacou women love each other is legend in Grenada, and so is their strength and their beauty*" (14), she puts it early, extending its legendary reach. Even Lorde's proper name is a respelling. It was in a library that the four-year-old first spoke; read to, she announced, "I want to read" (23); soon after, when she learned to make block letters she dropped the Y from AUDREY: "I did not like the tail of the Y hanging down." Lorde's mother wanted her to write AUDREY: "No deviation was allowed from her interpretations of correct" (24). Undeviating compliance was Lorde's mother's strategy for survival, a way not to be noticed by the white world, always assumed to be hostile. In her mother's arsenal of strength there was also the reverse strategy, of not noticing, not minding, blotting out threats to black existence. Lorde comes to embody both of these conflicting maternal stances; she refuses her propriety but nonetheless derives her new name from her mother's native language. So, too, taking Audre as her name, she does not depart from the alphabet that precedes her, though she pointedly refuses an appendage that would hang down from her textual embodiment. Likewise, scarcely a man figures in her biomythography of maternal inheritance.

"Zami" is not only a word used on Carriacou or Grenada for relations between women. It derives from French "les amies," eliding the "s" into the "z"-sound made in elision; through it a deviant, back-to-front mode of being singular plural is enunciated. Other Caribbean terms for female same-sex bonding cross other boundaries; "sodomite" or "man royal" are Jamaican locutions that masculinize, although not used for the male–male relations of battymen. "Mati" covers both male–male and female–female alliances in some locales.[4] In *Zami*, Lorde never actually calls herself by the name that titles the book. In it, she exists before the word, in the way in which she says her friends

---

4 For more details, see Goldberg, *Tempest in the Caribbean*, 53–79, as well as Makeda Silvera, "Man Royals and Sodomites: Some Thoughts on the Invisibility of Afro-Caribbean Lesbians," in Goldberg (ed.), *Reclaiming Sodom*, 95–105.

"were the hippies of the gay-girl circuit, before the word was coined," "trying to define ourselves as woman-identified women before we knew the word existed" (225). In these cases, "Black lesbian...defined...as doubly nothing" might broach a divide by way of double negation: "gay-girls were the only Black and white women who were talking to each other in this country in the 1950s, outside of the empty rhetoric of patriotism and political movements" (225). As much as for Cliff, ruin-nation is Lorde's position (she marks it by never capitalizing the name of any country). Political women in the 1950s opposed McCarthyism, but ignored racism and deplored lesbianism as "bourgeois and reactionary" (149). "Gay-girls," the locution for group self-naming most frequent in the book, is rejected by one of Lorde's white lovers who prefers "lesbian" (162), while Lorde winces when another says of lesbians "we're all niggers" (203). The few black gay-girls in the Greenwich Village bar scene "preferred the word 'dyke' and it seemed much more in charge of their lives to be dykes rather than gay-girls" (206).

In the opening pages of *Zami* that come even before the prologue that follows, Lorde seeks to name the source of her power, and lands on an "image of women flaming like torches" who "stand like dykes between me and the chaos" (3). "Dykes" is thus a chosen term, at last, at first, but precisely because it also is a pun, a bulwark outside oneself and against the chaos and yet the name of the group one joins to become a bulwark. "It is the image of women, kind and cruel, that lead me home" (3). "Kind and cruel" does not divide one group of women from another; so, too, Lorde's narrative charts her literal move away from her mother's house, built in defense against the world, to her return home: "Once *home* was a long way off, a place I had never been to but knew out of my mother's mouth" (256). "Zami" was not the only singular plural word uttered. Every divided, doubled word — every slap she administered — was also an education in a new mode of being, speaking, and writing.

Lorde comes to recognize that every place of belonging also is a place of threat. She can be with other gay-girls in the Bagatelle, although its doors are usually shut for much black clientele. The black lesbians in that scene would not recognize each other in Harlem, where race solidarity precludes sexual deviants.

Lorde's chosen gang of friends, "The Branded," include her on the unspoken agreement that her race never be mentioned. Lorde can comply: "I had no words for racism" (81), including lacking that word to describe her acceptance in that group of white outlaws. The young woman who prided herself on her knowledge is taken short when her first lover mentions Crispus Attucks, and Lorde realizes how her education (like Cliff's) has been a miseducation. *Zami* charts a pedagogic course marked by Lorde's affirmation of her sexuality, charting her affairs with women, black and white, fat and thin, bodily relations that take her beyond herself to the place of maternal enunciation:

> At home, my mother said, "Remember to be sisters in the presence of strangers." She meant white people....
> At St. Catherine's, they said, "Be sisters in the presence of strangers," and they meant non-catholics. In high school, the girls said, "Be sisters in the presence of strangers," and they meant men. My friends said, "Be sisters in the presence of strangers," and they meant the squares.
>
> But in high school, my real sisters were strangers; my teachers were racists; and my friends were that color I was never supposed to trust. (81)

Sisters (of various kinds) as strangers (of various kinds): Lorde named a collection of her writing that explores such non/belonging, *Sister Outsider*.[5] In *Zami* "different" is the word for this:

> *Being women together was not enough. We were different. Being gay-girls together was not enough. We were different. Being Black together was not enough. We were different. Being Black women together was not enough. We were different. Being Black dykes together was not enough. We were different.* (226)

---

5 Lorde, *Sister Outsider: Essays and Speeches* (Trumansburg, NY: Crossing Press, 1984).

Such insights have led Lorde to be hailed as an early theorist of intersectionality, but these differences are situational and mobile; they do not intersect so much as they pass by the very notion of a self where they might be imagined to cross: "Self-preservation warned some of us that we could not afford to settle for one easy definition, one narrow individuation of self.... We came to realize that our place was the very house of difference" (226). "To attempt a new language" (234), "a new spelling of my own name" (239), is the project.

* * *

I first read *Zami* some time in the late 1980s. I was spending the semester in Durham, NC, and occasionally sitting in on a graduate seminar that Eve Sedgwick and Michael Moon were teaching. I was in class the day Eve taught *Zami*. I still have tucked into my copy of the book the two poems of Lorde's Eve had xeroxed to open class discussion, "Coal" and "Ballad from Childhood," as well as my page of notes from the class. I've never been a good note-taker; my page lists topics broached, but fails to convey what I recall, a luminous presentation (I urged Eve to write it up; she demurred). Glancing now at those notes again, I see that the pages above have been my attempt, as has been the case with much of my writing since I first met and read Eve in the early- to mid-80s, of trying to find words for hers. She asked of *Zami* whether identity is a function of where and to whom one speaks; if categories of race, gender, and sexuality don't "interrupt" one another; how one becomes the "sujet supposé savoir" when knowledge is a scene of radical disjunctions and doubleness, culminating in the figure of the potent mother who kills (251), and how to survive that.

* * *

"Woman forever. My body, a living representation of other life older longer wiser. The mountains and valleys, trees, rocks. Sand and flowers and water and stone. Made in earth" (7).

AFTERWORD

After-Party: Sappho Meets Freud

by L.O. Aranye Fradenburg Joy

> Where does likeness stop? What does it delimit?
> — Goldberg, 63

After-parties happen when people don't want to go home (yet), have no place to go, feel the drive, can't bear to give each other up, want more intimacy, want more fluidity, want to meet new people. Most people who have read Sappho wish there were more Sappho. Jonathan Goldberg's book gives us more Sappho, and gives Sappho more afterlife, as have the writers and artists who appear in his own fragmentary, dis/seminal, hospitable responses to her writing and legend and multifarious reappearances. Goldberg's book is an act of generosity in more ways than one, formally, historically, thematically. It begins by declaring its affinity with Page duBois's stance that "Sappho baffles the categorical when it comes to sex and gender and sexuality" and that we "might reconsider the possibilities inherent in looking backwards differently...to the model of an ancient world in which the structures of heterosexual norms...had not yet been

---

* This essay is dedicated to the ever-festive, eternally-begetting Eileen A. Fradenburg Joy, and to Julie Carlson and Felice Blake, whose practices of and thinking about friendship are an unending source of delight and inspiration.

instituted in the name of the one god" (19). One of Goldberg's chief findings, e.g. in Willa Cather and Sarah Orne Jewett, in Michelle Cliff and Audre Lorde, in Patricia Highsmith's *The Price of Salt* and Todd Haynes's *Carol*, is Sapphist friendship, which may or may not be sexual, but is always alive to the embodied and embedded and hence erotic and loving and vulnerable nature of those who engage in it and share together their love of nectar and coming undone.[1] "I love the sensual," writes Sappho; "[f]or me this/and love for the sun/has a share in brilliance and beauty" (Fragment 9).[2]

Goldberg's Sappho participates in this aesthetic; it is beautiful, tactful, elliptical, redolent. And if it begins with duBois as Muse and interlocutor, it begins even earlier with Eve Sedgwick's writing, and "turns out," "in the end," to be also a love letter to Sedgwick and her speculations on identity and identification — "the pages above have been my attempt, as has been the case with much of my writing since I first met and read Eve in the early- to mid-80s, of trying to find words for hers" (132). Goldberg's Sappho is loving to many other women, and men, of many combinations and permutations (one of my favorite fragments, "*Sappho to Philaenis*," is on John Donne's "lesbianism"). Traces, hauntings, untranslatability, all the accoutrements of deconstruction familiar to readers of Goldberg's *oeuvre* act here as practices of finding, invitation, welcome, responsiveness. "The female–female desire" that Goldberg finds "goes unnamed

---

1 In his Fragment 5, "Histoire de Sappho," Goldberg figures "Anne Carson's analysis of sapphic love as a striving for a relationality that breaks through conventional limitations"; with/through his friends and colleagues, Joan de Jean and Karen Newman, he formulates Scudéry's representation of Sappho in this way: "Sapho, who declares she wants friends, not lovers, or wants a lover that is also a friend, wants 'to love innocently,'" that is, unconstrained by institutional forms and rituals (45). "Friend" is Willa Cather's word in Goldberg's Fragment 6, "Chance Encounters."

2 *Poems of Sappho*, translated by Julia Dubnoff (University of Houston), modified November 4, 2001, https://www.uh.edu/~cldue/texts/sappho.html. Fragment numbers are given in parentheses in the body of the text and refer to Dubnoff's translations unless otherwise indicated.

in Carson's *Eros the Bittersweet* has a name that is not one: Sappho, sapphism. It exceeds the usual binarism of gender since this female–female eros is not a matter of the same" (25). Goldberg's Fragment 3 takes up Pater's refusal, in an essay on Dionysius, to *decode* "one figure as another," insisting instead "on the paradox of sapphic bittersweet erotics, self-shattering loss coupled with maternal solicitude. He sees this sapphism realized in the figure of Bacchus" (30). Goldberg's "After-Party" returns and turns again to this coupling. "You know how we cared for you," says Sappho to her heartbroken friend — in other translations, "how we courted you," a semantic range this "After-Party" deeply appreciates) (Fragment 19); this is Dido's care also, as she burns for Aeneas, before he abandons her for epic.[3] Of course, self-shattering loss coupled with maternal solicitude is only a paradox when looked at from certain points of view; we might think of Kristeva's maternal *jouissance,* of Bracha Ettinger's "matrixial borderspace."[4] Both, it will be recalled, link the *jouissance* of pregnancy to split subjectivity or, more broadly with Ettinger, the experience of multiple partial self- and object-experiences capable of infinite reversal. We will return to this intimacy between care, hospitality, and arousal, on which every good party depends.

I wanted this book, because times are grim, and it has helped me feel better. Goldberg's Sappho is the result of a long series of invitations and rekindlings and tensions both put to rest and (re-)quickened, of the kinds of changing minds and relationships, care(s) and curiosities that also brought punctum books into being and that brought me and Sappho to punctum.

3   L.O. Aranye Fradenburg, *Staying Alive: A Survival Manual for the Liberal Arts,* edited by Eileen A. Joy (Brooklyn, NY: punctum books, 2013), 253.

4   The locus classicus for Kristeva on maternal *jouissance* is *Desire in Language: A Semiotic Approach to Literature and Art,* edited by Leon S. Roudiez, translated by Thomas Gora, Alice Jardine, and Leon S. Roudiez (New York: Columbia University Press, 1980), especially "Motherhood According to Giovanni Bellini," 237–71, the brilliance of which, for all its flaws, I still feel. For Ettinger, see *The Matrixial Borderspace,* edited by Brian Massumi, introduction by Griselda Pollock (Minneapolis: University of Minnesota Press, 2006).

Aficionados will know that the "punctum" in "punctum books" is the Barthesian punctum, an act/effect of transvaluation I have long admired in Goldberg's writing and in Sappho's. (The trope of "reversal," discussed below, can be used to similar effect, since it points to what lies between and outside the positions thus reversed.[5]) I think it is to be felt in Sapphic satire, though this is perhaps too obvious an example (but one that entertains me). When Sappho is satirizing her stupid brothers, she reverses the charges on epic:

> If [the gods]...have a whim, they make some henchmen
> fix it up, like those idiots in the Iliad.
> A puff of smoke, a little fog, away goes the hero.[6]

In another mood, it's a particular love that's worth far more than the massive stuff of epic: "[s]ome say an army of horsemen,/ some of footsoldiers,/ some of ships,/ is the fairest thing on the black earth,/ but I say it is what one loves" (Fragment 16). "*I say.*" One loves reading and writing and saying for their ability to link and hence transform minds and bodies and the strange non/human lives of signifiers. "[Y]ou must find your own quiet centre of life and write from that to the world that holds offices, and all society...in short, you must write to the human heart, the great consciousness that all humanity goes to make up" (71).[7] Love creates beauty, as Freud well knew; love spreads beauty over the body of "what one loves," in garlands,

---

5 Roland Barthes, *Camera Lucida: Reflections on Photography*, translated by Richard Howard (New York: Hill and Wang, 1981). My explanation is far from adequate!

6 "Charaxos and Larichos," translated by William Logan, *Poetry* (July/August 2016), reprinted by Poetry Foundation, https://www.poetryfoundation.org/poetrymagazine/poems/89724/charaxos-and-larichos.

7 Goldberg, in this volume: "I cite the passage as Edith Lewis does in *Willa Cather Living*; Lewis goes on to say, 'I am sure Willa Cather never forgot this letter...I think it became a permanent inhabitant of her thoughts'" (71).

leather, soft bedding, writing, feces.[8] "You know how we cared for you...

> For by my side you put on
> many wreaths of roses
> and garlands of flowers
> around your soft neck.
>
> And with precious and royal perfume
> you anointed yourself. (Fragment 19)

The power of *jouissance* to undo the "I" that "says" is well known, thanks to Sappho, and the power of her lyric voice lies precisely in its formal and forceful registration of transformation, wherein "I say" enters me (unforgettably) and makes me someone else, someone more sure, but less of a "one," different from what I was before, like the oak taken by the mountain winds. Loving Sappho's words loosens my limbs, "rattles" me, punctuates me. "My" identification, attachment, enchantment, is the paradoxical result of being struck, impressed, inhabited. Reading Goldberg, I recover the reach of enjoyment, its meaning for politics and sociality, its value, so depressed in US culture today, including the academy. I am given Sapphic friendship, in the form of relationships that remake the persons involved in them, whereby we become (aspects of) one another, because of our awareness of the other as capable of repose, suffering, pain, pleasure, joy, *jouissance*, expression, impression. Because languages of all kinds are necessary to

---

[8] Sigmund Freud, *Three Essays on the Theory of Sexuality* (1905), in *The Standard Edition of the Complete Psychological Works of Sigmund Freud, Volume VII (1901–1905): A Case of Hysteria, Three Essays on Sexuality and Other Works*, translated and edited by James Strachey, in collaboration with Anna Freud, assisted by Alix Strachey and Alan Tyson, 123–246 (London: Vintage, 2001), 150, on "overvaluation" of the sexual object. See also Elaine Scarry, *On Beauty and Being Just*, on the "phenomenon of unceasing begetting" sponsored by beauty (Princeton, NJ: Princeton University Press, 1999), 5.

these becomings, they too are ornamented, care-full — "I shall sing these songs / Beautifully / for my companions" (Fragment 3) — as the *troubadours* and *trobairitz*, the "finders," in one of Sappho's afterlives, would sing of the joy of singing. ("Le but n'est rien; le chemin c'est tout."[9])

Intersubjective psychoanalysis refers to the discourse co-created by analyst and analysand as the "third" (that goes beyond "two").[10] I link this to Goldberg–Carson's "something that exceeds" (24), which we might also imagine, perhaps to the surprise of some psychoanalysts, in the form of Lacan's "symbolic order," as a less personifying and enumerated way of naming the power of media to couple and uncouple and overtake the dyad and create chains and networks of / and companions.[11] Hence Carson–Goldberg's reflections on "that man" who seems to Sappho

> equal to the gods, the man who sits opposite you
> and close by listens
> to your sweet voice
> and your enticing laughter —
> that indeed has stirred up the heart in my breast.
> For whenever I look at you even briefly
> I can no longer say a single thing. (Fragment 31)

The now-venerable association of queerness with rhetoric and *vice-versa* (per-version, turning, troping, pre-posterousness) is legible as an aspect of primary process, Freud's term for the activity of the unconscious and the poetics of dreaming.[12]

---

9 Says Mr. Rosen in Willa Cather's "Old Mr. Harris," Goldberg, Fragment 6, "Chance Encounters," 57, in this volume.

10 Jessica Benjamin, "Beyond Doer and Done to: An Intersubjective View of Thirdness," *Psychoanalytic Quarterly* 73, no. 1 (2004): 5–46, https://doi.org/10.1002/j.2167-4086.2004.tb00151.x.

11 See Goldberg's Fragment 2, γλυκυπρον, on "the pairing of love and writing," 22, in this volume.

12 I refer to the work of Jonathan Dollimore, e.g. in *Sexual Dissidence: Augustine to Wilde, Freud to Foucault*, 2nd edition (Oxford: Oxford University Press, 2018), and that of Patricia Parker in *Literary Fat Ladies: Rhetoric, Gender, Property* (London and New York:

Primary process is, for Freud, how the semiotics of the body might reach out to the semiotics of the brain–mind, and again *vice-versa*, always *vice-versa*-ing, through the medium of drive theory, drives being not "raw" instincts, but their "representatives."[13] By such means, Freud thought, words like "he" and "she" could be dis/embodied, and cells could be excited by language. (The study of psychosomatic messengering is still new, but gaining strength in many circles of inquiry.[14]) Drive and desire ride the rails of sense-making. *Amor hereos*: Sappho makes beautiful the vicissitudes of the expressive drive entailed in joyful suffering.

> ...my tongue is frozen in silence;
> instantly a delicate flame runs beneath my skin;
> with my eyes I see nothing. (Fragment 31)

The dream literature of antiquity knew the mechanism of reversal, as Freud notes: "Artemidorus says: 'In interpreting the images seen in dreams one must sometimes follow them from the beginning to the end and sometimes from the end to the beginning.'"[15] The concept was important in early

---

Methuen, 1987) and "Virile Style," in *Premodern Sexualities*, edited by Louise Fradenburg and Carla Freccero, 199–223 (New York and London: Routledge, 1996).

13 Freud, "The Unconscious" (1915), in *The Standard Edition of the Complete Psychological Works of Sigmund Freud, Volume XIV (1914–1916): On the History of the Psycho-Analytic Movement, Papers on Metapsychology and Other Works*, translated and edited by James Strachey, in collaboration with Anna Freud, assisted by Alix Strachey and Alan Tyson, 159–215 (London: Vintage, 2001), e.g. 184.

14 See Marilia Aisenstein and Elsa Rappoport de Aisemberg, eds., *Psychosomatics Today: A Psychoanalytic Perspective* (New York: Routledge, 2018), especially e.g. the essay by Graeme J. Taylor, "Symbolism, Symbolization and Trauma in Psychosomatic Theory," 181ff.

15 Freud, *The Interpretation of Dreams* (1900), in *The Standard Edition of the Complete Psychological Works of Sigmund Freud, Volume IV (1900): The Interpretation of Dreams (First Part)*, translated and edited by James Strachey, in collaboration with Anna Freud, assisted

psychoanalysis: Freud reflects, in *The Interpretation of Dreams*, on the use of "reversal" in the "Introduction" to Alphonse Gaudet's *Sappho*, and remarks that "we derived our first hint of the existence of a dream-censorship" from analysis of a dream in which Freud feels "the greatest affection for my friend R., whereas and because the dream-thoughts called him a simpleton" (*ID*, 471). "Reversal" has had a surprisingly vigorous psychoanalytic afterlife, even in contemporary (North American) psychoanalysis, which does not typically display much fascination with Freud's First Topography, but, owing to its interest in intersubjectivity, has been known to turn to Ferenczi on occasion.[16] In fact, reversal has consistently been seen in psychoanalytic literature as one of the mind's most favored methods of transformation, at work in defense mechanisms, primary process, and counter / transference. The literature notes reversal of generations, of love into hate, of drive (in reaction-formation), of self-hurting and aggression, of activity into passivity, of sexual and gender identity, figure-ground, of libido from "in front" to "behind," container / contained, fear of life / fear of death, intrusion / evacuation, of pleasure into anxiety, to name just a few.

Freud explains:

> [R]eversal, or turning a thing into its opposite, is one of the means of representation most favoured by the dreamwork and one which is capable of employment in the most diverse directions. It serves in the first place to give

by Alix Strachey and Alan Tyson, ix–627 (London: Vintage, 2001), at 327n1, cited parenthetically hereafter as *ID*.

16 The "First Topography" is the name given to Freud's early mapping of the mind in terms of Consciousness, Preconsciousness, and the Unconscious, versus the Second Topography of ego, id, and superego. Freud's work on primary process was developed in connection with the First Topography. For Freud's discussion of Gaudet's *Sappho*, see *ID*, 284ff. Sándor Ferenczi discusses reversal mechanisms in *First Contributions to Psychoanalysis*, translated by Ernest Jones, *The International Psycho-Analytical Library* no. 45 (1916; reprinted London: The Hogarth Press and the Institute of Psycho-Analysis, 1952), e.g. "reversal of affect" at 148.

expression to the fulfilment of a wish in reference to some
particular element of the dream-thoughts. "If only it had
been the other way round!" (*ID*, 326)

One might add: "if only I could have / be both sides of the coin, like Tiresias"; or, "if I could turn this around, my experience of life would double"; or, "the gender-marking I have endured, let it end now, let me have been both and neither"; or, "let me turn back time, to the time when I was neither." (Reversal is a prominent symptom in Freud's writing on "Dora's case."[17])

Freud remarks of the end of "the interesting Up and Down dream" (*ID*, 326) that it featured a reversal of "difficulty going upstairs as described in [Gaudet's] Sappho.... In Sappho the man carried a woman who was in a sexual relation to him; in the dream-thoughts the position was reversed, and a woman was carrying a man...the reference was...to [a]...wet-nurse bearing the weight of [an]...infant in her arms.... Just as the author of the novel, in choosing the name 'Sappho,' had in mind an allusion to Lesbian practices, so too the pieces of the dream that spoke of people 'up above' and 'down below' alluded to phantasies of a sexual nature" (*ID*, 322); "the end of the dream made a simultaneous reference to Sappho and to the wet-nurse" (*ID*, 326). The dream changes a man into a woman and a woman into a man, and an adult into a baby and a baby into an adult. We might therefore add to "phantasies of a sexual nature" phantasies and even unconscious memory-traces of maternal and fetal *jouissance*, of uterine life, of being borne and born, of "carrying" in all senses: "You know how we cared for you"; "[e]vening, thou that bringst all that bright morning scattered, / thou bringst the sheep, the goat, and the child back to its mother" (Fragment 92). The evening, of course, also brings friends together in parties.

---

17 Sigmund Freud, *Fragment of an Analysis of a Case of Hysteria* (1905), in *The Standard Edition of the Complete Psychological Works of Sigmund Freud, Volume VII (1901–1905): A Case of Hysteria, Three Essays on Sexuality and Other Works*, translated and edited by James Strachey, 1–122 (London: Hogarth Press, 1953), 27–8.

The lyric is often choric in Sappho's writing and in her afterlife (cf. Goldberg on *Carol / The Price of Salt*); "Cleis the belovedest / whom I cherish more than all Lydia or lovely [Lesbos]" (Fragment 82); it twins the mother and the daughter (Cleis–Cleis), the indistinction and fluidity of person in uterine existence, of gender too, not only in the early experience of the embryo but for the whole time in which what will later be named a "male" body is not distinguishable from what will be named a "female" body.[18] This sharing of experience — thus far, both "men" and "women" begin their lives inside the bodies of "women" who may or may not identify as or "be" such — is articulated, one way or another, throughout Goldberg's *Sappho*, which ends like this: sometimes "men are not women, women not men, but what is 'between' is perhaps nonetheless the same" (46). The dreamer of "the Sappho dream" (who dreams in relation to Gaudet's version of Sappho), moreover, turns "round in relation to his brother," inhabitant of the same womb (*ID*, 287f.), whose contempt for that brother is legible as the unconscious "opposite" of his desire for him (reversals, perhaps, of *phobia* into *philia*): "[in] his earlier years [he] had greatly tormented his elder brother, to whom he had a homosexual attachment" (*ID*, 158); "It is remarkable to observe," Freud writes in this discussion of reversal, "how frequently reversal is employed precisely in dreams arising from repressed homosexual impulses" (*ID*, 326).

"This turning of a thing into its opposite is made possible by the intimate associative chain which links the idea of a thing with its opposite in our thoughts" (*ID*, 470). These intimate associative chains, which we might imagine as neural pathways, are created by lived experience, by our embodied embeddedness in history, on the "black earth," channeling also the lived experiences of the past, the ancestors, life in the "matrixial borderspace," enacting (or defeating) the futures sought by our "wishes," indeed, our prayers: "…my weeping: it and all care let buffeting winds bear away."[19] "Like any other kind of dis-

---

18 I refer to Kristeva's work on the "chora," in *Desire in Language*, 6–7, 281ff.
19 Lobel-Page 37 / 14D / Wharton 17 / Cox 17, in Sean B. Palmer, *Sap-*

placement," reversal "can serve the ends of the censorship, but it is also frequently a product of wish-fulfillment" (*ID*, 470), as is, indeed, the censorship itself, not least in its later conceptualization as the "superego," which so commonly, in our experience, sickens from its idealizations and the demonizations that are their "opposites." Ambivalence, polyamory — "I am of two minds," writes Sappho — and the intimacy of *phobia* and *philia*, love and hate, admiration and scorn, are legible here in terms of the reversal of "affects attaching to dream-thoughts" (*ID*, 470), a reminder that the taxonomic impulses of contemporary affect studies can tempt us to underemphasize the plasticity and interconnectivity of affect.[20] "And all the wrong he did before, loose it," writes Sappho of her now not so much annoying as "soul-ravaged," tormented and tormenting brother. She prays to "Kypnis and Nereides,"

> Make him a joy to his friends,
> a pain to his enemies and let there exist for us
> not one single further sorrow.[21]

Make it the other way round. Turning it around, turning one's back, turning it down, or up.

That we suffer from our affects and that they can also transform into their "opposites," or into their friends and neighbors, are obvious points, but (as Goldberg / Carson bring out in their reflection on "bittersweet"), reading Sappho defamiliarizes them, in the same way that (for me) reading Freud does, on, e.g., the fixity *and* lability of libido he sees in the process of mourning. *Amor hereos* again, yes, in the form of Sappho's

---

pho's Poems, http://inamidst.com/stuff/sappho/.

20 "Libido and disgust would seem to be associatively linked"; Freud, Letter from Freud to Fliess, November 14, 1897, in *The Complete Letters of Sigmund Freud to Wilhelm Fliess, 1887–1904*, edited by Jeffrey Moussaieff Masson, 278–82 (Cambridge, MA: Belknap Press, 1985), at 280.

21 Lobel-Page 5 / Voigt 5 / Gallavotti 23 / Diehl 25 / Bergk, in Palmer, *Sappho's Poems*.

recognition of the power of language to summon, transform, disperse, "metabolize" the vicissitudes of desire.

> And oftentime when
> our beloved, wandering abroad, calls to mind
> her gentle Atthis, the heart devours her
> tender breast with the pain of longing; and
> she cries aloud to us to come thither.[22]

This is the power of Sapphic friendship, of crying aloud to those who love us or at least can hear us, and this is also the power of psychoanalysis and the endless work of mourning. Remembering can make us suffer, but can also be a balm to the spirit, a "blessing," *bracha* in Hebrew, as when we say, "may her memory be a blessing."

> Weeping many tears, she left me and said,
> "Alas, how terribly we suffer, Sappho.
> I really leave you against my will."
>
> And I answered: "Farewell, go and remember me.
> You know how we cared for you.
>
> If not, I would remind you
> ... of our wonderful times.
>
> For by my side you put on
> many wreaths of roses
> and garlands of flowers
> around your soft neck.
>
> And with precious and royal perfume
> you anointed yourself. (Fragment 19)

"She *said*," "I *answered*." The talking, singing, conversing, partying cure helps us to change and at the same time to remember, to remember in order to change, to change so that we

---

22 Lobel-Page 96 / Voigt 96 / Diehl 98, in Palmer, *Sappho's Poems*.

can bear our memories. Parties are prescribed for melancholy; in *Troilus and Criseyde,* neither the death-driven Troilus nor the narrator can bear the idea, but Pandarus's attempts to make Criseyde's absence bearable for Troilus are part of a therapeutic tradition as old as Sappho's world, if a bit more problematic in the world of the "one god":

> ...with al myn herte I thee beseche,
> Un-to thy-self that al this thou foryive...
> And lat us caste how forth may best be drive
> This tyme, and eek how freshly we may live...
> Rys, lat us speke of lusty lyf in Troye
> That we han lad, and forth the tyme drive;
> And eek of tyme coming us reioye,
> That bringen shal our blisse now so blyve...
> Go we pleye us in som lusty route.[23]

Let's remind ourselves of the good things we've enjoyed. Party on; more elegantly, let us go on becoming and, as Elaine Scarry would say, begetting.[24]

The discourses of *amor hereos,* medical, philosophical, historical, artistic, conversational, friendly, are meant, by turns, or at once, to heal, express, enjoy pain. These discourses variously foreground the intimacy of pain and healing, the *pharmakon,* and nowhere is this more evident than in the history of Sapphic writing. The *razos* and *vidas,* also phenomena of "unceasing begetting," were the lovingly expansive medieval after-parties that celebrated the songs of the *troubadours* and the *trobairitz,* but they also tried to make sense of the notorious contradictions of a lyric creativity that ranged from praise of the cunt to

---

23 Geoffrey Chaucer, *Troilus and Criseyde,* in *The Riverside Chaucer,* edited by Larry Benson, 3rd edition, 471–586, (Boston, MA: Houghton-Mifflin, 1987), V, 386–402. Cf. Glending Olson, *Literature as Recreation in the Later Middle Ages* (Ithaca, NY: Cornell University Press, 1986), and Stanley Jackson, *Care of the Psyche: A History of Psychological Healing* (New Haven, CT: Yale University Press, 1999).

24 See note 8 above.

praise of the Virgin in the *oeuvre* of a "single" singer, and were unafraid, like Sapphic satire, to reverse the charges on Imaginary masculinist puffery, melancholic, epic, or otherwise. *Amor hereos*, as I have argued in *Sacrifice Your Love*, is part of the genealogy of psychoanalysis, as it is of queerness.[25] It requires the queering of "health" and "happiness"—anathema to the mental eugenics of today's "positive" psychologists.[26] And psychoanalysis, consistently forgetting its queerness, is today celebrating it more so, if the wonderful transformations ongoing at my own institute, the New Center for Psychoanalysis in Los Angeles, are any indication.

I turn now to the "analytic functions" that, according to Borgogno and Vigna-Taglianti, "create the affective inter-psychic conditions that will enable the transmission of the emotional alphabet needed to master...lived experience."[27] Following Ferenczi, Winnicott, and Bion, they argue for an "inversion of roles", a "role-reversal" that undoes the "dissociation within the analyst of the infantile and suffering part of the patient."[28] Through role reversal, the analyst "personifies and literally 'embodies' *in vivo,* within the unconscious dialogue, not only the parents but the suffering child in relation—through the patient—to a truly inadequate and traumatic parent."[29] *Both*

---

25 L.O. Aranye Fradenburg, *Sacrifice Your Love: Chaucer, Psychoanalysis, Historicism* (Minneapolis: University of Minnesota Press, 2001), 3, 10.

26 For one truly terrifying example, see Martin E.P. Seligman, *Learned Optimism: How to Change Your Mind and Your Life* (New York: Vintage Books, 2006). I am grateful to Oksana Yakushko for sharing her thoughts about positive psychology with me (personal communication).

27 Franco Borgogno and Massimo Vigna-Taglianti, "Role Reversal: A Somewhat Neglected Mirror of Heritages of the Past," *American Journal of Psychoanalysis* 68, no. 4 (December 2008): 313–24, at 313.

28 Borgogno and Vigna-Taglianti, "Role Reversal," 313.

29 Borgogno and Vigna-Talianti, "Role Reversal," 314, 320n3, citing Sándor Ferenczi, "Confusion of Tongues between Adults and the Child," in *Final Contributions to the Problems and Methods of Psychoanalysis*, edited by Michael Balint, translated by Eric Mosbacher et al. (London: Hogarth Press, 1955), 156–7; *The Clinical Diary of*

generational "opposites" (as noted previously, a common reversal in the dream-work) must be embodied in the analyst as they are in the patient, just as, for Ferenczi and later Frankel, "identification with the aggressor" can even in "normality" lead to "identifying collusions both with the 'aggressor' and with the 'victim.'"[30] "I am of two minds," perhaps more; or, again, the intimacy of *phobia* and *philia*. For patients to be able to re-member their unspeakable because unknown histories, "the analyst will also have to be both the child the patient has been, and the child who is able...in all senses to make himself heard."[31] Ferenczi draws our attention to "a certain phobia of us analysts as to...identification with the suffering child and his vulnerability,"[32] the phobia also legible in positive psychology, to say nothing of those premodernists who have sought to empty *amor hereos* of its affective significance and wisdom.

Identification with the suffering child, further, involves (as Borgogno and Vigna-Talianti note, following Winnicott[33]) the summoning up of something real within the analyst, perhaps of something Real, perhaps of the something Real that Bracha Ettinger locates at the level of uterine experience and the extraordinary *experiencing* of the suffering and *jouissance* of the other of whom "I," who is no "I," am also a part, and potentially in reverse, somatically as well as in every other way. I give Bracha Ettinger, who is a blessing to me, my penultimate words: "[T]he matrix is an unconscious borderspace of co-emergence and co-fading in the partial dimension, and *metramorphosis*

Sándor Ferenczi, edited by Judith Dupont (Cambridge, MA: Harvard University Press, 1988); and Jay Frankel, "Exploring Ferenczi's Concept of Identification with the Aggressor: Its Role in Trauma, Everyday Life, and the Therapeutic Relationship," *Psychoanalytic Dialogues. The International Journal of Relational Perspectives* 12, no. 1 (2002): 101–39, https://doi.org/10.1080/10481881209348657.

30 Borgogno and Vigna-Taglianti, "Role Reversal," 320n3.
31 Borgogno and Vigna-Taglianti, "Role Reversal," 316.
32 Borgogno and Vigna-Taglianti, "Role Reversal," 316.
33 Borgogno and Vigna-Taglianti, "Role Reversal," 314, referring to D.W. Winnicott, "Mirror-Role of Mother and Family in Child Development," in *Playing and Reality* (London: Tavistock, 1971), 111–8.

is its *noncastrative* process of passability and conductivity, repression and dispersal that creates transformations-in-differentiation and 'makes sense' beyond distinct representations and discourse," in the space of reversibility.[34] The experience of this matrixial borderspace does not just remain within all of us but reaches out and enables us to wish each (other) well.

---

34 My emphasis on "noncastrative." Bracha Lichtenberg-Ettinger, "The Feminine/Prenatal Weaving in Matrixial Subjectivity-as-Encounter," *Psychoanalytic Dialogues* 7, no. 3 (1997): 367–405, at 367, https://doi.org/10.1080/10481889709539191.

Bibliography

Aisenstein, Marilia, and Elsa Rappoport de Aisemberg, eds. *Psychosomatics Today: A Psychoanalytic Perspective.* New York: Routledge, 2018.

Allen, D.C. "Donne's 'Sappho to Philaenis.'" *English Language Notes* 1, no. 3 (March 1964): 188–91.

Baker, Deborah Lesko. *The Subject of Desire: Petrarchan Poetics and the Female Voice in Louise Labé.* West Lafayette, IN: Purdue University Press, 1996.

Barthes, Roland. *Camera Lucida: Reflections on Photography.* Translated by Richard Howard. New York: Hill and Wang, 1981.

Bartlett, Neil. "Fallen Angel." *The Guardian,* October 7, 2005. https://www.theguardian.com/artanddesign/2005/oct/08/art.

———. *Solo Voices: Monologues 1987–2004.* London: Oberon Books, 2005.

———. *A Vision of Love Revealed in Sleep (Part Three).* In *Gay Plays,* edited by Michael Wilcox, Volume 4, 87–112. London: Methuen Drama, 1990.

———. *Who Was That Man? A Present for Mr Oscar Wilde.* London: Serpent's Tale, 1988.

Bates, Catherine. "The Lesbian Phallus in *Sapho to Philaenis.*" In *Masculinity, Gender and Identity in the English Renaissance Lyric,* 216–58. Cambridge: Cambridge University Press, 2007.

Bechdel, Alison. *Are You My Mother?: A Comic Drama.* New York: Houghton Mifflin Harcourt, 2012.

———. *The Essential Dykes to Watch Out For.* New York: Houghton Mifflin Harcourt, 2008.

Benjamin, Jessica. "Beyond Doer and Done to: An Intersubjective View of Thirdness." *Psychoanalytic Quarterly* 73, no. 1 (2004): 5–46. https://doi.org/10.1002/j.2167-4086.2004.tb00151.x.

Bersani, Leo. *Thoughts and Things*. Chicago: University of Chicago Press, 2015.

Borgogno, Franco, and Massimo Vigna-Taglianti. "Role Reversal: A Somewhat Neglected Mirror of Heritages of the Past." *American Journal of Psychoanalysis* 68, no. 4 (December 2008): 313–24.

Brody, Richard. "'Carol' Up Close." *The New Yorker*, November 30, 2015. https://www.newyorker.com/culture/richard-brody/carol-up-close.

Buonarroti, Michelangelo. *The Poems*. Edited and translated by Christopher Ryan. London: J.M. Dent, 1996.

Carson, Anne. *Eros the Bittersweet*. London: Dalkey Archive Press, 1998.

———. *If Not, Winter: Fragments of Sappho*. New York: Vintage Books, 2003.

Castle, Terry. "Always the Bridesmaid, Never the Groom." In *Boss Ladies, Watch Out! Essays on Women, Sex, and Writing*, 167–79. New York: Routledge, 2002.

Cather, Willa. *24 Stories*. Edited by Sharon O'Brien. New York: Meridien, 1988.

———. *Not Under Forty*. Lincoln: University of Nebraska Press, 1988.

———. *Obscure Destinies*. New York: Vintage, 1974.

———. *The Selected Letters of Willa Cather*. Edited by Andrew Jewell and Janis Stout. New York: Knopf, 2013.

———. *The World and the Parish: Willa Cather's Articles and Reviews, 1893–1902*. Edited by William M. Curtin. 2 volumes. Lincoln: University of Nebraska Press, 1970.

Chaucer, Geoffrey. *Troilus and Criseyde*. In *The Riverside Chaucer*, edited by Larry Benson, 471–586. 3rd edition. Boston: Houghton-Mifflin, 1987.

Clark, Kenneth. *Looking at Pictures*. New York: Holt, Rinehart and Winston, 1960.

Clarke, Cheryl. *The Days of Good Looks: The Prose and Poetry of Cheryl Clarke, 1980 to 2005*. New York: Carroll & Graf, 2006.

———. *Living as a Lesbian*. New York: A Midsummer Night's Press; Berkeley, CA: Sinister Wisdom, 2014.

Cliff, Michelle. "Caliban's Daughter: The Tempest and the Teapot." *Frontiers: A Journal of Women Studies* 12, no. 2 (1991): 36–51. http://dx.doi.org/10.2307/3346845.

———. *The Land of Look Behind: Prose and Poetry*. Ithaca, NY: Firebrand Books, 1985.

Clover, Carol J. *Men, Women, and Chainsaws: Gender in the Modern Horror Film*. Princeton, NJ: Princeton University Press, 1997.

Cruise, Colin. *Love Revealed: Simeon Solomon and the Pre-Raphaelites*. London: Merrell, 2005.

Da Vinci, Leonardo. *The Notebooks of Leonardo da Vinci*. Edited by Edward McCurdy. New York: George Braziller, 1958.

———. *Selections from the Notebooks of Leonardo da Vinci*. Edited by Irma A. Richter. London: Oxford University Press, 1952.

Davis, Nick. "The Object of Desire." *Film Comment* 51, no. 6 (Nov/Dec 2015): 30–5.

DeJean, Joan. *Fictions of Sappho, 1546–1937*. Chicago: University of Chicago Press, 1989.

Dollimore, Jonathan. *Sexual Dissidence: Augustine to Wilde, Freud to Foucault*. 2nd edition. Oxford: Oxford University Press, 2018.

Donne, John. *The Poems of John Donne*. Edited by Herbert J.C. Grierson. Oxford: Clarendon Press, 1912.

Douglas, Lord Alfred. "Two Loves." In *Sexual Heretics: Male Homosexuality in English Literature from 1850 to 1900*, edited by Brian Reade. London: Routledge and Kegan Paul, 1970.

DuBois, Page. *Sappho*. London: I.B. Tauris, 2015.

———. *Sappho is Burning*. Chicago: University of Chicago Press, 1995.

Empson, William. *Some Versions of Pastoral*. 1935. Reprinted London: Chatto & Windus, 1950.

Ettinger, Bracha. *The Matrixial Borderspace*. Edited by Brian Massumi. Introduction by Griselda Pollock. Volume 28 of *Theory Out of Bounds*. Minneapolis: University of Minnesota Press, 2006.

Faderman, Lillian. *Surpassing the Love of Men: Romantic Friendship and Love between Women from the Renaissance to the Present.* New York: William Morrow, 1981.

Ferenczi, Sándor. *The Clinical Diary of Sándor Ferenczi.* Edited by Judith Dupont. Cambridge, MA: Harvard University Press, 1988.

———. "Confusion of Tongues between Adults and the Child." In *Final Contributions to the Problems and Methods of Psycho-analysis,* edited by Michael Balint, translated by Eric Mosbacher et al. London: Hogarth Press, 1955.

———. *First Contributions to Psychoanalysis.* Translated by Ernest Jones. *The International Psycho-Analytical Library* no. 45. 1916. Reprinted London: The Hogarth Press and the Institute of Psycho-Analysis, 1952.

Flatley, Jonathan. *Like Andy Warhol.* Chicago: University of Chicago Press, 2017.

Fradenburg, L.O. Aranye. *Sacrifice Your Love: Chaucer, Psychoanalysis, Historicism.* Minneapolis: University of Minnesota Press, 2001.

———. *Staying Alive: A Survival Manual for the Liberal Arts.* Edited by Eileen A. Joy. Brooklyn, NY: punctum books, 2013.

Frankel, Jay. "Exploring Ferenczi's Concept of Identification with the Aggressor: Its Role in Trauma, Everyday Life, and the Therapeutic Relationship." *Psychoanalytic Dialogues: The International Journal of Relational Perspectives* 12, no. 1 (2002): 101–39. https://doi.org/10.1080/10481881209348657.

Freud, Sigmund. *Fragment of an Analysis of a Case of Hysteria.* 1905. In *The Standard Edition of the Complete Psychological Works of Sigmund Freud, Volume VII (1901–1905): A Case of Hysteria, Three Essays on Sexuality and Other Works,* translated and edited by James Strachey, 1–122. London: Hogarth Press, 1953.

———. *The Interpretation of Dreams.* 1900. In *The Standard Edition of the Complete Psychological Works of Sigmund Freud, Volume IV (1900): The Interpretation of Dreams (First Part),* translated and edited by James Strachey, in collaboration with Anna Freud, assisted by Alix Strachey and Alan Tyson, ix–627. London: Vintage, 2001.

———. *Leonardo da Vinci and a Memory of His Childhood.* Translated by Alan Tyson. New York: W.W. Norton, 1964.

———. Letter from Freud to Fliess, November 14, 1897. In *The Complete Letters of Sigmund Freud to Wilhelm Fliess, 1887–1904,* edited by Jeffrey Moussaieff Masson, 278–82. Cambridge, MA: Belknap Press, 1985.

———. *Three Essays on the Theory of Sexuality.* 1905. In *The Standard Edition of the Complete Psychological Works of Sigmund Freud, Volume VII (1901–1905): A Case of Hysteria, Three Essays on Sexuality and Other Works,* translated and edited by James Strachey, in collaboration with Anna Freud, assisted by Alix Strachey and Alan Tyson, 123–246. London: Vintage, 2001.

———. "The Unconscious." 1915. In *The Standard Edition of the Complete Psychological Works of Sigmund Freud, Volume XIV (1914–1916): On the History of the Psycho-Analytic Movement, Papers on Metapsychology and Other Works,* translated and edited by James Strachey, in collaboration with Anna Freud, assisted by Alix Strachey and Alan Tyson, 159–215. London: Vintage, 2001.

Gallagher, Lowell. *Sodomscapes: Hospitality in the Flesh.* New York: Fordham University Press, 2017.

Goldberg, Jonathan. Introduction. In *Reclaiming Sodom,* edited by Jonathan Goldberg, 1–22. New York: Routledge, 1994.

———. *Melodrama: An Aesthetics of Impossibility.* Durham, NC: Duke University Press, 2016.

———. *Tempest in the Caribbean.* Minneapolis: University of Minnesota Press, 2004.

Greek Lyric I: Sappho and Alcaeus. Translated by David A. Campbell. Loeb Classical Library. Cambridge, MA: Harvard University Press, 1982.

Gubar, Susan. "Sapphistries." *Signs: Journal of Women in Culture and Society* 10, no. 1 (Autumn 1984): 43–62. https://doi.org/10.1086/494113.

Halpern, Richard. *Shakespeare's Perfume: Sodomy and Sublimity in the Sonnets, Wilde, Freud, and Lacan.* Philadelphia: University of Pennsylvania Press, 2002.

Hartt, Frederick. *Michelangelo Drawings.* New York: Abrams, 1970.

Harvey, Elizabeth D. *Ventriloquized Voices: Feminist Theory and English Renaissance Texts*. London: Routledge, 1992.

Haynes, Todd. *Far From Heaven; Safe; and Superstar, the Karen Carpenter Story: Three Screenplays*. New York: Grove, 2003.

H.D. *Collected Poems 1912–1944*. Edited by Louis Martz. New York: New Directions, 1983.

———. *Notes on Thought and Vision & The Wise Sappho*. San Francisco, CA: City Lights, 1982.

Highsmith, Patricia [Claire Morgan]. *The Price of Salt*. 1952. Reprinted New York: W.W. Norton, 1990.

Homestead, Melissa. "The Composing, Editing, and Publication of Willa Cather's *Obscure Destinies* Stories." *Scholarly Editing: The Annual of the Association for Documentary Editing* 38 (2017). http://scholarlyediting.org/2017/essays/essay.homestead.html.

———. "Willa Cather, Edith Lewis, and Collaboration: The Southwestern Novels of the 1920s and Beyond." *Studies in the Novel* 45, no. 3, Special Issue: The Work of Willa Cather: Creation, Design, and Reception (Fall 2013): 408–41.

Hovey, Jaime. *A Thousand Words: Portraiture, Style, and Queer Modernism*. Columbus: Ohio State University Press, 2006.

Jackson, Stanley. *Care of the Psyche: A History of Psychological Healing*. New Haven, CT: Yale University Press, 1999.

Jewett, Sarah Orne. *The Country of the Pointed Firs and Other Stories*. Preface by Willa Cather. Garden City, NY: Doubleday and Co., 1954.

———. *Letters of Sarah Orne Jewett*. Edited by Annie Fields. Boston, MA: Houghton Mifflin, 1911.

Kristeva, Julia. *Desire in Language: A Semiotic Approach to Literature and Art*. Edited by Leon S. Roudiez. Translated by Thomas Gora, Alice Jardine, and Leon S. Roudiez. New York: Columbia University Press, 1980.

Labé, Louise. *Complete Prose and Poetry*. Edited by Deborah Lesko Baker. Chicago: University of Chicago Press, 2006.

Lachman, Edward. "Edward Lachman Shares His Secrets For Shooting Todd Haynes' 'Carol.'" *Indiewire*, December 3, 2015. https://www.indiewire.com/2015/12/edward-lachman-shares-his-secrets-for-shooting-todd-haynes-carol-48627/.

Lewis, Edith. *Willa Cather Living: A Personal Record.* 1953. Reprinted Lincoln: University of Nebraska Press, 2000.

Lichtenberg-Ettinger, Bracha. "The Feminine / Prenatal Weaving in Matrixial Subjectivity-as-Encounter." *Psychoanalytic Dialogues* 7, no. 3 (1997): 367–405. https://doi.org/10.1080/10481889709539191.

Lorde, Audre. *Sister Outsider: Essays and Speeches.* Trumansburg, NY: Crossing Press, 1984.

———. *Zami: A New Spelling of My Name.* Freedom, CA: Crossing Press, 1982.

Love, Jean O. "*Orlando* and Its Genesis: Venturing and Experimenting in Art, Love, and Sex." In *Virginia Woolf: Revaluation and Continuity: A Collection of Essays,* edited by Ralph Freedman, 189–218. Berkeley: University of California Press, 1980.

Majumdar, Robin, and Allen McLaurin, eds. *Virginia Woolf: The Critical Heritage.* London: Routledge & Kegan Paul, 1975.

Martial. *Epigrams.* Translated by D.R. Shackleton Bailey. 3 volumes. Loeb Classical Library. Cambridge, MA: Harvard University Press, 1993.

———. Epigram LXVII, Book VII. Translated by Gillian Spraggs. 2006. http://www.gillianspraggs.com/translations/philaenis.html.

Maxwell, Lynn. "Woman as World: The Female Microcosm / Macrocosm in Shakespeare and Donne." In *This Distracted Globe: Worldmaking in Early Modern Literature,* edited by Marcie Frank, Jonathan Goldberg, and Karen Newman, 190–211. New York: Fordham University Press, 2016.

Menon, Madhavi. *Wanton Words: Rhetoric and Sexuality in English Renaissance Drama.* Toronto: University of Toronto Press, 2004.

Michelet, Jules. *Ouevres de M. Michelet.* 3 volumes. Brussels: Meline, 1840.

Moon, Michael. Review of *Fun Home: A Family Tragicomic,* by Alison Bechdel. *Guttergeek: The Discontinuous Review of Graphic Narrative,* September 2006. http://guttergeek.com/archives/2006/page78/funhome/funhome.html.

Moore, Lisa L. "A Lesbian History of the Sonnet." *Critical Inquiry* 43, no. 4 (Summer 2017): 813–38. https://doi.org/10.1086/692380.

O'Brien, Sharon. "'The Thing Not Named': Willa Cather as a Lesbian Writer." *Signs: Journal of Women in Culture and Society* 9, no. 4 (Summer 1984): 576–99. https://doi.org/10.1086/494088.

———. *Willa Cather: The Emerging Voice*. Oxford: Oxford University Press, 1987.

O'Donovan, Rocky. "Reclaiming Sodom." In *Reclaiming Sodom*, edited by Jonathan Goldberg, 247–8. New York: Routledge, 1994.

Olson, Glending. *Literature as Recreation in the Later Middle Ages*. Ithaca, NY: Cornell University Press, 1986.

Ovid. *Heroides and Amores*. Translated by Grant Showerman. London: William Heinemann, 1921.

Palmer, Sean B., ed. *Sappho's Poems*. http://inamidst.com/stuff/sappho/.

Parker, Patricia. *Literary Fat Ladies: Rhetoric, Gender, Property*. London and New York: Methuen, 1987.

———. "Virile Style." In *Premodern Sexualities*, edited by Louise Fradenburg and Carla Freccero, 199–223. New York and London: Routledge, 1996.

Pater, Walter. *Greek Studies: A Series of Essays*. London: Macmillan, 1911.

Prettejohn, Elizabeth. "Solomon's Classicism." In *Love Revealed: Simeon Solomon and the Pre-Raphaelites*, edited by Colin Cruise, 39–45. London: Merrell, 2005.

Prins, Yopie. *Victorian Sappho*. Princeton, NJ: Princeton University Press, 1999.

Reid-Pharr, Robert. *Black Gay Man: Essays*. New York: New York University Press, 2001.

Sackville-West, Vita. *The Letters of Vita Sackville-West to Virginia Woolf*. Edited by Louise DeSalvo and Mitchell A. Leaska. New York: William Morrow, 1985.

Sappho. "Charaxos and Larichos." Translated by William Logan. *Poetry* (July/August 2016). Reprinted by Poetry Foundation. https://www.poetryfoundation.org/poetrymagazine/poems/89724/charaxos-and-larichos.

———. *Poems of Sappho*. Translated by Julia Dubnoff. University of Houston. Modified November 4, 2001. https://www.uh.edu/~cldue/texts/sappho.html.

Scarry, Elaine. *On Beauty and Being Just*. Princeton, NJ: Princeton University Press, 1999.

Schenkar, Joan. *The Talented Miss Highsmith: The Secret Life and Serious Art of Patricia Highsmith*. New York: St. Martin's, 2009.

Scudéry, Madeleine de. *The Story of Sapho*. Translated by Karen Newman. Chicago: University of Chicago Press, 2003.

Seligman, Martin E.P. *Learned Optimism: How to Change Your Mind and Your Life*. New York: Vintage Books, 2006.

Shannon, Laurie. "'The Country of Our Friendship': Jewett's Intimist Art." *American Literature* 71, no. 2 (June 1999): 227–62.

Silvera, Makeda. "Man Royals and Sodomites: Some Thoughts on the Invisibility of Afro-Caribbean Lesbians." In *Reclaiming Sodom*, edited by Jonathan Goldberg, 95–105. New York: Routledge, 1994.

Smith-Rosenberg, Carroll. "The Female World of Love and Ritual: Relations Between Women in Nineteenth-Century America." *Signs: Journal of Women in Culture and Society* 1, no. 1 (Autumn 1975): 1–29. https://doi.org/10.1086/493203.

Solomon, Simeon. Letter, 1886. In *Sexual Heretics: Male Homosexuality in English Literature from 1850 to 1900*, edited by Brian Reade. London: Routledge and Kegan Paul, 1970.

———. *A Vision of Love Revealed in Sleep*. In Simon Reynolds, *The Vision of Simeon Solomon*. Stroud: Catalpa Press, 1984.

Stokes, Adrian. *Michelangelo: A Study in the Nature of Art*. London: Tavistock Publications, 1955.

Traub, Valerie. "Recent Studies in Homoeroticism." *English Literary Renaissance* 30, no. 2 (March 2000): 284–329. https://doi.org/10.1111/j.1475-6757.2000.tb01173.x.

———. *The Renaissance of Lesbianism in Early Modern England*. Cambridge, UK: Cambridge University Press, 2002.

Winkler, Jack. "Gardens of Nymphs: Public and Private in Sappho's Lyrics." In *Reflections of Women in Antiquity*, edited by Helene P. Foley, 63–90. New York: Gordon and Breach Science Publishers, 1981.

Winnicott, D.W. "Mirror-Role of Mother and Family in Child Development." In *Playing and Reality,* 111–8. London: Tavistock, 1971.

Wittig, Monique, and Sande Zeig. *Lesbian People: Material for a Dictionary.* London: Virago, 1980.

Woolf, Virginia. *The Diary of Virginia Woolf.* Edited by Anne Olivier Bell. 5 volumes. New York: Harcourt, 1977–84.

———. *The Letters of Virginia Woolf.* Edited by Nigel Nicolson and Joanne Trautmann. 6 volumes. New York: Harcourt, 1975–80.

———. *Moments of Being.* Edited by Jeanne Schulkind. New York: Harcourt, 1985.

———. *Orlando: A Biography.* Edited by Maria DiBattista. New York: Harcourt, 2006.

———. *A Room of One's Own.* Edited by Susan Gubar. New York: Harcourt, 2005.

———. *To the Lighthouse.* New York: Harcourt, 1981.

"W. dreams, like Phaedrus, of an army of thinker-friends, thinker-lovers. He dreams of a thought-army, a thought-pack, which would storm the philosophical Houses of Parliament. He dreams of Tartars from the philosophical steppes, of thought-barbarians, thought-outsiders. What distance would shine in their eyes!"

— Lars Iyer

www.ingramcontent.com/pod-product-compliance
Lightning Source LLC
Chambersburg PA
CBHW060836190426
43197CB00040B/2654